Bought 9/23/2021

Graduation

Celebrating 400 years of personal achievement at the University of Edinburgh

Jean Grier and Mary Bownes

ISBN 978-0-9534945-9-0
Published by the University of Edinburgh

Professor Sir Timothy O'Shea, Principal and Vice-Chancellor 2002-2017.

Dedication

This booklet is dedicated to our Principal and Vice-Chancellor Professor Sir Timothy O'Shea to recognise him on his retirement as Principal of the University of Edinburgh.

In choosing the subject of this book we wanted to look at something which Sir Timothy had both shaped and valued as part of the University calendar. Since he joined the University in 2002, making him the longest serving Vice-Chancellor since Sir Edward Appleton (Principal from 1948 – 1965), Sir Timothy has not only led the University further and further up the global rankings and brought in a huge amount of research income, he has also been aware of the importance of our built environment and the impact the University has on the city. He has also changed the culture of the University to be more inclusive and open.

Sir Timothy recognises that one of the most important days of the year is when students graduate following an extensive period of study at the University of Edinburgh. As a result he carefully shaped the modern day ceremony to be a wonderful mix of the pomp and ceremony expected of such an event but with a friendly human touch. Furthermore as the number of students graduating increases, many ceremonies are run rather than fitting more and more students into each ceremony, so that the event remains special to each graduate and their families and friends. That we are back in the McEwan Hall following a major refurbishment is also testament to another of Sir Timothy's main interests which is the history of the University and the careful custodianship of its many iconic buildings. Beautiful as many of these buildings are, they are often unfit for current expectations and safety requirements, and careful development and redevelopment will be an issue for many years to come.

Introduction

In this slim volume, we will show how the personal achievements of students have been recognised by the University at different stages in our four hundred year history.

Starting with a very brief history of the University, we will look at how the early 'laureation' ceremonies took place around the city; at how the University grew from a handful of students in 1583 to the world-renowned institution it is today; at some of the early international input to the University and at how our graduates have contributed globally. Looking at the magnificent McEwan Hall, we will investigate the philanthropy which made it possible in the first place, the design principles behind it, and describe the huge refurbishment project which has recently been completed.

The graduation ceremonies are the true focus of this book, and so we will look at how these have developed over the years – at the robes and gowns, the inclusion of music in the ceremonies, the recognition of the achievements of each individual graduate but also of those to whom honorary degrees and other awards are made – and through all of this, the importance of our alumni to the University and wider community across the world, once the ceremony itself is over.

The Bedellus, Drew Laven, ushers the Principal to the platform.

6 The early years of the University

The University was founded in 1583 as the Tounis College or 'Town's College'.

At this point, there were just two universities in England – Oxford and Cambridge. Scotland, however, already had three universities – St Andrews (founded in 1413), Glasgow (1451) and Aberdeen (1495), but all of these were set in bishops' burghs and rooted in the Catholic Church. Edinburgh's Tounis College was to be different, educating ministers for the post-Reformation Protestant Kirk, as well as training men for the administration of the capital city. The population of Edinburgh was over 14,000 by this time, making it far bigger than St Andrews, Aberdeen or even Glasgow; the royal court was largely resident at the Palace of Holyroodhouse; and meetings of both Parliament and the General Assembly were usually held in Edinburgh. Edinburgh was therefore an important place, and needed a university of its own.

The college began its life on the site it still occupies, and where Old College now stands. In the early years of the college, teaching was carried out in an assortment of buildings belonging to the town council. The history of those buildings is interesting in itself – premises associated with the Kirk o' Fields Church, the scene of the murder of Henry Stuart, Lord Darnley, in 1567. As second husband of Mary, Queen of Scots, Lord Darnley was staying in lodgings at Kirk o' Fields to visit his wife when a massive explosion destroyed much of the building. His body was found close by – not killed in the explosion, but murdered in some other way. The mystery of his murder has never been solved. A few years later, the town council made the buildings on the site available for the newly-formed college.

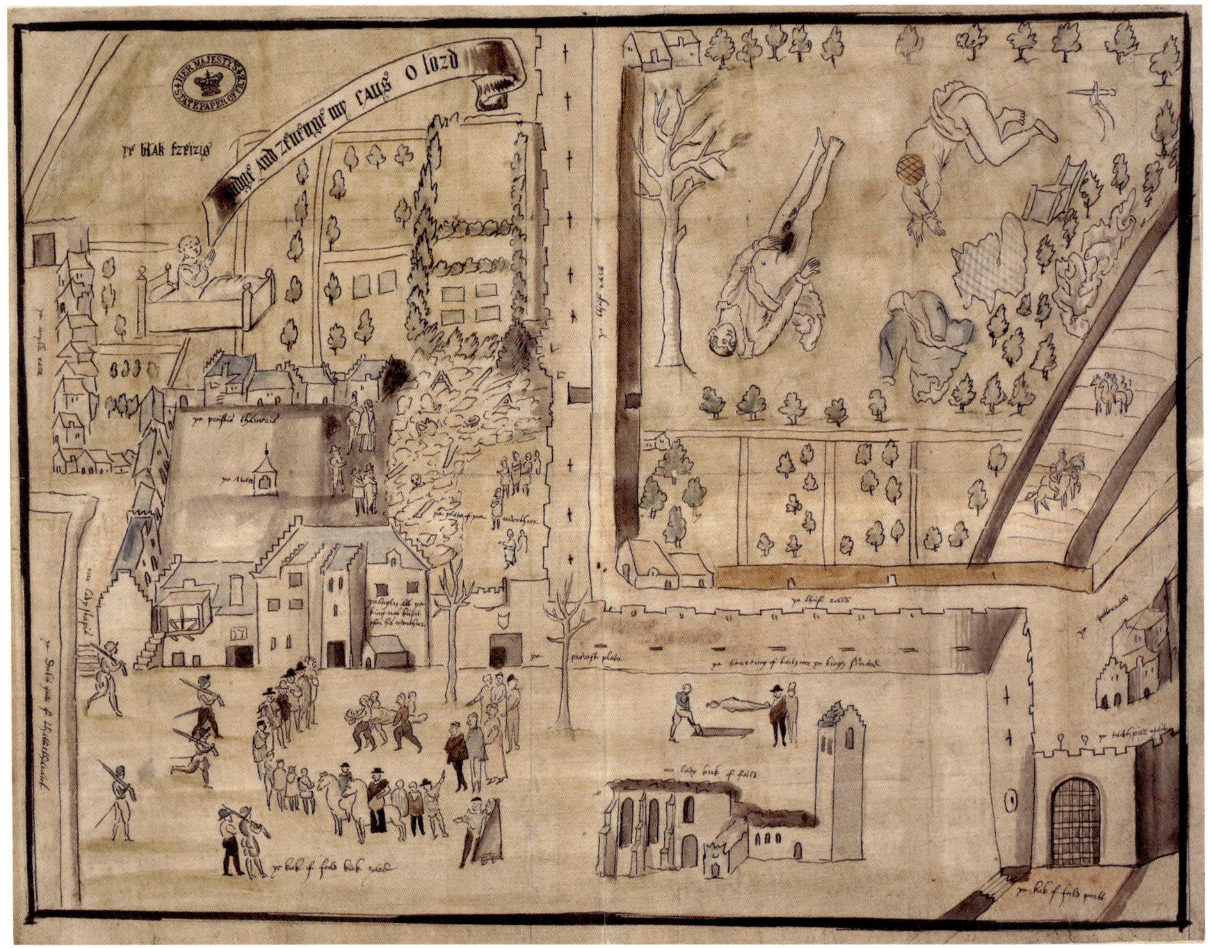

This contemporary drawing depicts the scene in 1567 when the prebendaries' lodgings were blown up and Lord Darnley was killed.

An unknown number of boys turned up when the college opened in October 1583, but many were turned away again a few days later when they failed a Latin exam. The average age of students in the early years of the University was just 14, and they were taught by a single teacher, or 'regent', who led them through all subjects in all years until their studies were completed. In many ways, the early college was more like a school than what we now think of as a university.

Despite a shaky start – for example, the college had to be evacuated to Linlithgow during 1585 due to an outbreak of the plague in Edinburgh – student numbers grew, additional regents were appointed, and new buildings were acquired or built on the Old College site over the next 150 years. However, by the late 18th century, it was clear that the University could not continue to function in such an assortment of semi-derelict buildings, and plans for Old College were developed.

Robert Adam designed the fine new buildings but died before there was much to show for his efforts. Shortage of funds put the project on hold, and it was re-started only after the then-Principal had gone on a begging trip to London for more money. William Playfair was commissioned to modify Adam's plans and introduce some economies, and though there were many further delays and modifications, Old College was essentially completed by around 1840.

The foundation stone for Old College was laid in 1789.

R Rowand Anderson's dome was added in 1886, and topped by 'the golden boy' statue in 1889.

By this time, the University had around 3,500 students, and was teaching a wide range of subjects from astronomy through to zoology, but still with a serious focus on divinity and around half the total student population studying medicine – in other words, with an emphasis on professional training.

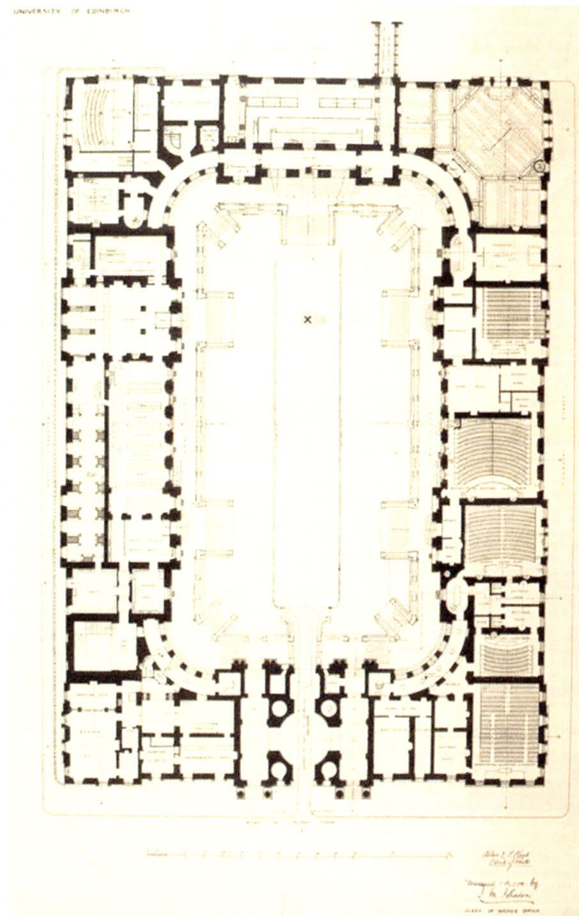

After Adam's death, Playfair redesigned Old College.

Known as the 1617 building, the lower floor was used as a common hall and laureations took place in it. The upper floor was a library. By the time these drawings were done, the building was in a poor state and Old College was being built around it.

'Golden Boy' on top of the dome of Old College.

By 1950, the number of women studying had increased to the point where they had their own union in George Square.

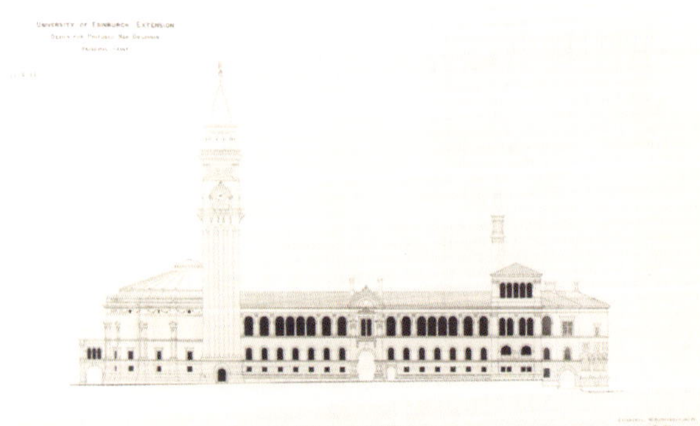

Anderson's design for the new medical school included a campanile which was never built.

The development of the modern University

In 1858, control of the University was taken away from the town council for the first time, and the University Court was established – an arrangement which is still in place today.

Student numbers continued to increase and there was much discussion nationally about raising the entrance age and defining the boundary between 'school' and 'university'. Greater specialisation saw the creation of professorships in subjects such as Sanskrit, political economy and Celtic. All teaching was squeezed into Old College, and expanded premises became crucial. A Buildings Extension Scheme was set up in 1883 and a plot of land was bought adjacent to the Meadows. Over the next 50 years, the University went on to acquire the old High School buildings in Infirmary Street, Minto House and other buildings in Chambers Street, and moved a number of departments into houses in George Square.

The Buildings Extension Scheme oversaw fundraising of £60,000 through public subscription, and the architect Robert Rowand Anderson won the competition to design the 'new buildings'. The first of these was to be the new medical school. The city's infirmary had moved from Infirmary Street to Lauriston Place in 1879, and siting the new medical school buildings adjacent to it was a logical step.

An act of parliament in 1889 paved the way for the admission of women to the University, though our first female students were not admitted until 1892 and their numbers were not significant until the First World War.

Unlike the college-based structure of the other universities in England and Scotland, Edinburgh had been largely non-residential, with students from beyond the city taking lodgings. This was to change in the early 20th century, with the establishment in George Square of the first halls of residence – Masson House for women, and Cowan House for men.

Students in one of the modern social areas.

Development continued as the University bought a green-field site at Liberton in 1919, and the science subjects were gradually relocated there as buildings were completed – chemistry in 1922, zoology in 1929 and geology in 1932, with others following thereafter to the King's Buildings. The second half of the 20th century saw a massive expansion in university provision across the UK, including the establishment of a number of new universities and the creation of polytechnics. Government funding was also channelled into the existing universities, and at Edinburgh much of this was deployed around the George Square area with the building of the Appleton Tower, Main Library, David Hume Tower and George Square Lecture Theatre. Mergers also took place – for example, with New College (Divinity) in 1935, the Veterinary College (Royal (Dick) School of Veterinary Studies) in 1951, Moray House School of Education in 1998, and Edinburgh College of Art in 2011.

As a result of all these developments, the University is now a community of around 37,000 students and 12,000 staff from 160 different countries. Students study at all levels, with the number of postgraduate students growing especially. Students and staff are engaged in world-leading research, and the University is a major employer within the region. It makes a significant contribution in the local, national and international arenas, and is consistently ranked one of the top universities in the world. It has come a long way since its establishment over 400 years ago in a group of second-hand buildings, and we fully expect it to continue to be innovative for many years to come.

The Joseph Black Building (Chemistry), shown here in around 1948, was the first to open at the King's Buildings, in 1922.

Studying in the Main Library.

Graduations and laureations

The early students didn't 'graduate' as such. After four years of study, the magistrands or final year students left University following a laureation ceremony, held in one of the town's churches or, later, in a hall on the Old College site.

This came after what appears to have been a gruelling series of examinations, some of them oral and some written, taken over several days. First year students or 'baijans' were examined by being given a passage of text in Scots which they then had to translate into Latin. Second year students ('semibajans') had to translate Latin into Greek before analysing the text publicly in front of all the professors. The 'bachelars' or third year students were examined on a number of topics, depending on their ages. Finally, the 'magistrands' or fourth year students had to gather before the Principal and regents the night before the 'publick disputation on the Theses'. They had to sign the Confession of Faith along with an undertaking to be dutiful to the college and masters.

Trinity Collegiate Church, later demolished to make way for Waverley Station, was used for early laureations.

Dressed in black gowns similar to those worn by their professors, the magistrands were then arranged by the Principal in two circles in a rough order of merit. The students who had done less well in the preceding exams were arranged in a line, apparently to ensure that they were not called upon to answer anything in public. Candidates were then called forward by name to receive their degree from the Principal. The regent of the class prepared a 'thesis' – presumably an essay of some description – which was then read out and debated, or in the case of mathematics, chalked up on a board for discussion. The ceremonies appear to have involved a public question and answer session, all conducted in Latin – apart from the bits which were conducted in Greek or Hebrew – with some students proposing a thesis and others defending or attacking it. How much the audience might have understood is debatable, but a large gathering of local ministers, advocates and bailies (town councillors) came to hear these debates – and possibly to select young men for a future career, almost treating these events like a modern recruitment fair.

Laureations appear to have been grand affairs, with benches and carpets provided for distinguished guests, and soldiers employed as door-keepers, but during the seventeenth century laureations became less and less frequent. One reason for this was that it was necessary to take an oath – the Confession of Faith – at laureation, and religious turmoil meant that Presbyterians were unwilling to take the oath when the Episcopalians were in power, and vice versa. However, another factor seems to have been the timing of the ceremonies.

As soon as teaching finished, students were keen to return to their homes. Then, as now, returning to Edinburgh for a ceremony some weeks or months later was probably seen by some students as an unnecessary expense or a distraction from other activities. In 1633 the town council proposed fining students who did not stay on for laureation, but this proposal does not appear to have been implemented. There was also some disquiet from parents, who were concerned that magistrands were listed at the beginning of the graduation theses in order of merit. Arguments about who was better than whom led to this practice being replaced by alphabetical listing until 1643, when there was a return to listing magistrands in order of merit.

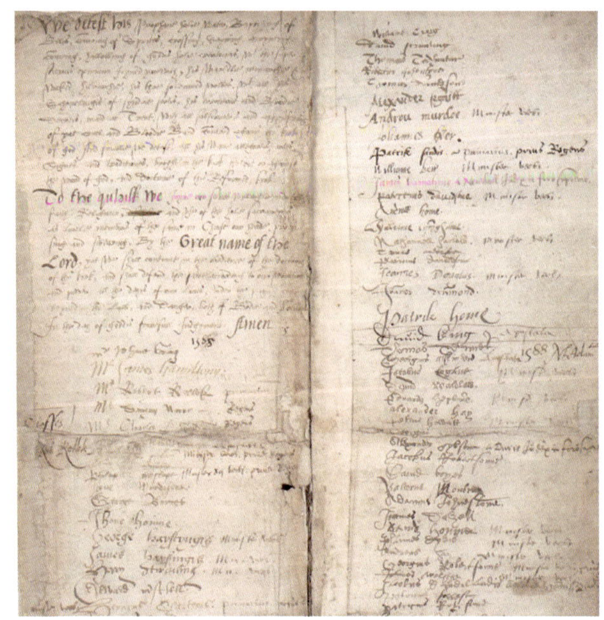

This laureation album records the University's first graduates in 1587.

These various difficulties seem to have led to laureations becoming private affairs rather than public spectacles. Graduation theses in the first half of the 17th century typically list about 30 students each year. First year student numbers exceeded 100 for the first time in 1662. Total student numbers at this time were probably around 300, but numbers fluctuated for many reasons – in 1645, for example, the University was evacuated to Linlithgow due to yet another plague outbreak in Edinburgh, and it is also likely that parents withdrew their sons from study at difficult times like this.

It is very difficult to gain an accurate picture of student numbers in the early years of the University as students paid their fees direct to their regent, but drop-out rates seem to have been very high, with up to 60 percent of students failing to complete their studies. Equally, some sources suggest that many students possibly 'dropped in' again and – with little of the current concept of a linear progression from first year through to graduation – it is impossible to track graduates against admission numbers with any certainty, or even to be certain how many students enrolled in any given year.

By the 1820s, boys were on average only 15 or 16 when they enrolled as students. There was still no real concept of 'graduation' as such. Students could collect class certificates, and those with ambition could compete for a class prize, but the majority of students simply picked the classes they wished to go to, without any concept of following a set curriculum or completing a degree as such. Law students were generally working in offices during the day and attending a few classes, and wealthy students might follow a year or two of philosophy or classics to give them a rounded education. But class sizes, especially in arts subjects, were large – around 150 – 200 students. The Senatus introduced the BA degree in 1842, with lower requirements than the MA and completion within three years rather than four, but graduation rates were still very low. In the 1860s, only around a dozen students a year graduated with the MA, and fewer still with the BA.

The situation was slightly different for those studying medicine. By 1726, candidates for medical degrees were required to produce evidence that they had studied for three years and had attended clinical lectures at a hospital. They also had to prepare a thesis and undergo an oral exam, though even in medicine, graduation was not particularly valued – of the 400 or so students studying medicine, only around 20 graduated with the MD degree. It was possible at that time to become a doctor or a surgeon with few, if any, qualifications. But the University made concerted efforts to encourage completion and graduation, and these efforts began to have an impact. In 1859, only 87 students graduated, of whom 62 were medical. In 1890-1, 98 students graduated with an MA, 36 with a BSc and 19 with an LLB, while 250 received the medical degree. Graduation was not yet the aim of every student, but was on the way to becoming the norm. It is against this background that plans for a 'great hall' for the University gained momentum.

Laureation ceremonies were held in St Giles for some time in the early years of the University. The University carol service was also held in the Cathedral while the McEwan Hall was undergoing its recent refurbishment.

Greyfriars Kirk was one of several churches which housed University services, including laureations. It is still used today for some University services.

Built in 1642, this building provided space for a much needed 'common hall' – used thereafter for graduations – with a library above.

Timeline

1583
Tounis College founded

1587
47 Graduates initially, and thereafter around 25 a year on average

1606
Edinburgh referred to as a 'city' for the first time

1617
First purpose-built library completed on Old College site, including a 'common hall'

1630s
Graduating numbers average around 36 a year

1642
'New library' built on Old College site

1659
45 Students graduate

1669
70 students enrol in first year

1688
First use of the title 'University' for Edinburgh

1690s
Student numbers in serious decline following religious upheavals

1701-26
Reform of the University, with a new four-year curriculum

1726
Medical faculty established

1727
First student society established (the Royal Medical Society)

1749
First American graduate from Edinburgh (John Moultrie)

1750
Student numbers around 600, 300 of them in medicine

1768
Around 6-700 students, plus 21 professors

1789
Foundation stone laid for Old College

1793
751 Students in total, 427 studying medicine

1825
Student numbers over 2,000, of whom 60% are studying medicine

1842
BA degree introduced

1844
Student numbers fall to 1,056, with just 370 studying medicine

1855
First Chinese graduate from Edinburgh (Dr Wong Fun)

1858
University becomes independent of the town council; first rector appointed

1858
General Council – comprising all graduates plus professors – established

1859
First African graduate from Edinburgh (Dr James Africanus Beale Horton)

1860s
About a dozen students a year graduate with the MA; fewer take the BA

1861
Student numbers 1,462, 543 of them studying medicine

1874
Plans developed for new medical school

1884
Students' Representative Council (SRC) founded

1884
Expansion in student numbers to 3,423, with 1,736 in medicine

1885
Student numbers peak for a time at 3,602 this year

1886
Old College is completed by the addition of the dome

1888
Work begins on the McEwan Hall

1892
First women students admitted

1893
First women students graduate, having completed most of their studies through an external association linked to the University

1897
McEwan Hall opens

1914
Around 1,000 students a year admitted by the start of the First World War

1919
Site acquired at Liberton for King's Buildings campus

1935
New College, a divinity school established in 1843, becomes part of the University

1937
Student numbers 4,139, of whom 3,132 are men and 1,007 are women; the growth in overall numbers has been mainly due to the increase in female students

1881-1931
Significant increase (40%) in the population of the Lothians

1942
Site for Pollock Halls of Residence given by Sir Donald Pollock

1948
Incorporation of the Edinburgh Dental School

1948
Student numbers 5,640

1951
Merger with the Royal (Dick) School of Veterinary Studies

1953
HRH The Duke of Edinburgh inaugurated as Chancellor

1953
Student numbers 4,537

1960s
Major expansion and development, especially around George Square

1960
Student numbers 5,963

1970
Student numbers 9,368

1988
Student numbers 10,403

1990
Student numbers 18,000

1998
Merger with Moray House College of Education; student numbers rise to 20,000

2005
Student numbers 24,468

2009
Student numbers 28,394

2011
Merger with Edinburgh College of Art; student numbers 31,336

2011
Inauguration of HRH The Princess Royal as Chancellor

2014
McEwan Hall closes for refurbishment

2015
Student numbers 37,416

2016
Student numbers 36,491

2017
McEwan Hall reopens

Student numbers and the growth of the University

While medicine was just one of the disciplines on offer at the University, it was an extremely important factor in the University's overall growth, accounting for around half the total number of students from the 1750s through to the 1820s. The proportion of medical students dipped a little in the 1840s as the number of students studying humanities grew, but significant expansion from the 1870s onwards saw a return to a high proportion of medical students and major pressures on teaching space.

Current student numbers

Student body by college

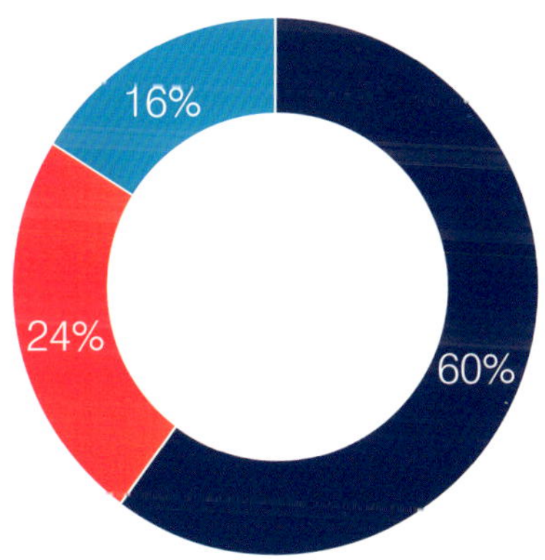

Arts, Humanities & Social Sciences		22,453
Science & Engineering		9,128
Medicine & Veterinary Medicine		5,835
	Total	**37,416**

Student body by domicile on entry

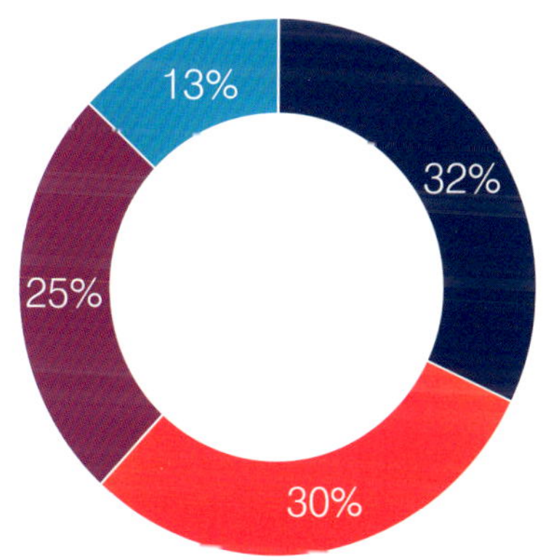

Scotland		12,172
International		11,340
Other UK		9,178
Other EU and Cyprus		4,726
	Total	**37,416**

The 'new buildings' – an architectural overview

The development of new medical school buildings, to be located adjacent to the new Royal Infirmary in Lauriston Place, required a major fund-raising effort.

The sum of £165,000 for purchase of the site and for buildings works came from public subscriptions, with a further £88,000 from government grants. The site had gradually been cleared – including the demolition of the Edinburgh Poor-House in Teviot Row – prior to its acquisition by the University, and The Scotsman newspaper announced the architectural competition in September 1874, saying that 'The buildings to be erected are to comprise a completely appointed Medical School, as also a College Hall, suitable for important academical gatherings'. In 1875 it was announced that Robert Anderson, an Edinburgh-based architect, had won the competition. Anderson – who later styled himself R Rowand Anderson – adopted what he called 'the Cinquecento style'. His plans incorporated the medical school and hall as required, plus an Italianate campanile.

By 1880, the anatomy department was occupying its new premises, complete with museum, and work was proceeding well on the rest of the medical school. Medical student numbers increased dramatically, however, almost doubling in the space of seven years – a recognition, perhaps, of the excellent teaching at Edinburgh – and plans had to be adjusted to allow for the increased numbers, jeopardising the resources available for the great hall and campanile which had been an integral part of Anderson's design for the 'new buildings'. William McEwan was to enable the building of the hall which now bears his name; the campanile, however, was never built.

William McEwan and the McEwan Hall

The statue of William McEwan stands at the foot of the staircase.

William McEwan founded the Fountain Brewery in Edinburgh in 1856. Of about 40 breweries in Edinburgh at the time, McEwan's became one of the most successful – and he also developed a significant export trade across the British Empire, making use of his father's shipping line.

In addition to a strong business sense, William McEwan also clearly believed in 'giving back'; in 1886 he became Member of Parliament for Central Edinburgh, and over the years he gave significant sums of money to the city. His greatest gift, however, was to be the McEwan Hall.

The absence of a 'University Hall' had been a problem for many years, and in 1874, when the campaign for the new buildings was launched, the 'degradation' of being reduced to hiring a hall for great occasions was mentioned. Comparisons with Oxford's Sheldonian Theatre were made, and those attending a public meeting to launch the fund-raising campaign were assured that the University of Edinburgh would 'shortly stand possessed of a Hall of Assembly which has no parallel elsewhere'. It was, however, to be over 20 years before the hall was completed, but it was indeed magnificent.

In 1884 the University had launched its Tercentenary Appeal, and William McEwan made a generous initial donation. In 1886 he intimated that he was willing to contribute a further £40,000 to enable the University to achieve its great hall, but he increased that figure later to £115,000. Calculating the modern day equivalent of any historic sum of money produces wildly different figures, but at the very least, Mr McEwan's gift would equate to £11.3 million today; and calculated on another recognised basis, it could equate to as much as £175 million.

Work started on the hall in 1888. It is semi-circular (or built on a D-plan), with two steeply-raked galleries. Built in Early Italian Renaissance style, the façade is flanked by towers housing the spiral staircases to the two galleries. The sculpture over the door depicts a graduation ceremony, and the inscription records McEwan's generosity.

William McEwan hoped that the ceremonial hall would be made available to the people of Edinburgh, and though it has had some use as a public hall, its primary function has always been as a space for University events – graduations of course, but also concerts, public lectures, and as an examination hall. It is also used for University open days, and for events such as the welcome ceremony for new students.

In their gratitude for William McEwan's generosity, the University awarded him the honorary degree of Doctor of Laws at the opening ceremony of the McEwan Hall on 3 December 1897.

The tympanum over the main entrance to the McEwan Hall depicts a graduation ceremony.

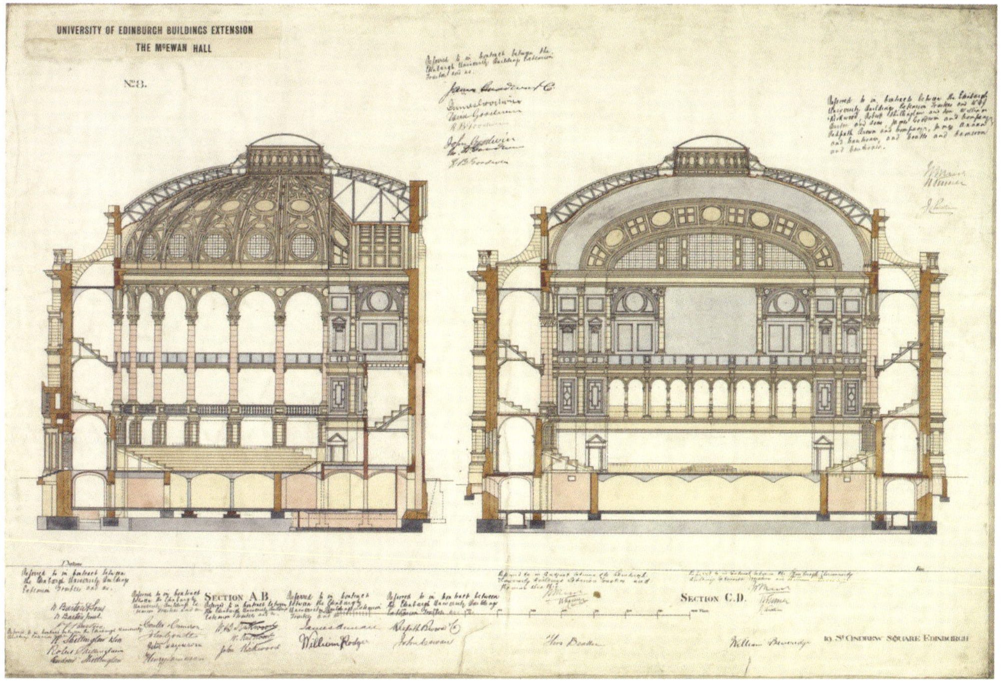

R Rowland Anderson's drawings for the McEwan Hall.

The McEwan Hall soon after its completion.

William Palin's designs for the interior

The handsome exterior of the McEwan Hall hints at a magnificent interior, but even so, most people are surprised by the opulence of the decorations within the hall.

William Palin was apprenticed to Josiah Wedgwood and Sons before gaining a scholarship to the Royal College of Art in London. He was recommended to the committee overseeing the Buildings Extension Scheme, and at the age of 31 he embarked on the designs for the murals. Building of the hall itself was finished by 1894, but the lavish interior decorations commissioned by McEwan took almost another four years to complete.

Palin's scheme conveys something of how the ideal of a university was viewed at the time. The vast dome is divided by ribs into 15 panels. At the base of each of these is a seated female figure, all but two of whom hold an instrument relevant to the academic discipline they represent. The lower part of the dome lists famous names associated with the University – including Thomas Carlyle, James Hutton and Joseph Black. On the next level down is the biblical inscription 'Wisdom is the principal thing, therefore get wisdom, and with all thy getting, get understanding. Exalt her and she shall bring thee to honour'.

Over the proscenium arch is a complex composition on the theme of the Temple of Fame. This depicts over 80 philosophers and students ascending the steps. At the top are the goddesses of Science, Art and Literature. Literature, in the centre, has a quill in her hand and on her knee is the Book of Fame.

Two smaller panels at each side of the platform show (to the right) Minerva in the grove of Academia. In the group of figures to her left, William McEwan (with arms crossed and long white beard) is proffering the gift of his hall. To the left of the arch Fame is crowning Success. Other desirable attributes, such as Perseverance, Intelligence, Imagination and Experience, are also portrayed.

This quotation from the Scriptures sits below the dome.

Writer Thomas Carlyle is one of a number of famous alumni immortalised in the decorations.

The University's collections include Palin's original designs for the murals, and the recent refurbishment works in the hall have allowed a close-up inspection of them for the first time in many years.

Scaffolding during the refurbishment work allowed close-up inspection of Palin's murals.

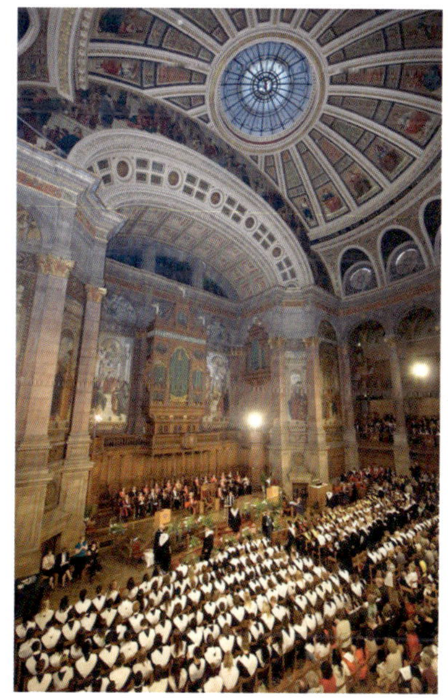

Views of the refurbished hall, and during a graduation ceremony prior to refurbishment.

The recent refurbishment and redevelopment

In 2014, the McEwan Hall was closed to allow for a major programme of refurbishment and redevelopment.

During this time, the University hired the Usher Hall from the City Council for the graduation ceremonies. Conceived of in 1896, the year before the McEwan Hall opened, the Usher Hall was not completed until 1914. Design developments in the intervening years give the Usher Hall a very different 'feel' to the McEwan Hall. This changed the format of graduation ceremonies slightly, though the main change – welcomed by many students – was the fact that the much larger Usher Hall meant that graduands could apply for up to four tickets for their guests, rather than the two they had been restricted to in the McEwan Hall. Fire safety regulations brought in during the 20th century closed the upper gallery at the McEwan Hall, reducing the seating available. This shortage of space has been addressed by the refurbishments, which allow us to use the upper gallery once more and increase the capacity to 1,800.

As other major events in the University calendar – most notably, perhaps, the welcome ceremony in September and the carol service in December – have in the past seen more people turning up than can be accommodated, regaining access to the upper gallery is a huge benefit of the refurbishment.

The refurbishment was necessary for a number of reasons. Firstly, routine maintenance on a building of this scale and age is an ongoing commitment, and significant repair works were required to the roof and other areas. But it was also realised that the limitations of the McEwan Hall meant that it was underused, and so the opportunity was taken to develop it as a resource capable of fulfilling a number of functions. The refurbishment has created new spaces for conferences, exhibitions, events and education. The main hall has been restored, making it a spectacular multi-functional space in a unique and splendid Victorian setting. A new entrance hall provides greatly improved visitor facilities, and renovation of the basement area has transformed the provision for robing areas for graduations and other events. Disabled access has been addressed with the provision of a lift, and the upper tiers of seating have been brought back into use. The main public access to the hall is now through a new entrance way in Bristo Square.

Externally, stonework has been repaired and the landscaping of Bristo Square has been redesigned to make it more accessible and safe, while also opening up its potential as a public space for activities and performances. All this work should enable greater public use of this iconic and historic building, fulfilling the original vision of Sir William McEwan, and shared by current staff at the University.

The Usher Hall was used for ceremonies during 2015 and 2016 while the McEwan Hall was undergoing refurbishment.

The refurbishment works to the McEwan Hall were extensive, including much landscaping work.

An impression of the scale of the refurbishment project can be gained from the quantity of scaffolding.

Cleaning of the décor has allowed Palin's murals to be fully appreciated.

This sectional drawing shows the improved access and basement.

Perseverance and Intelligence.

From the world To Edinburgh...

The University now has students from over 160 countries, and 40 percent of our students come from beyond the UK.

While our proportion of international students has changed over the years, Edinburgh has been a sought-after destination for students for over 250 years – despite considerable difficulties over travel, in some cases. The University's first American graduate, John Moultrie, spent 32 days crossing the Atlantic to take up his place at Edinburgh, and those coming from China, India or Africa will also have experienced lengthy and perilous journeys. Even the journey from London could take a week or more prior to the building of the railways. Physically reaching Edinburgh is much easier for current students, but considerable planning may need to go into visa applications before they can take up their places here.

Many of these pioneering students went on to make notable contributions in the world. Benjamin Rush, one of about a hundred Americans who enrolled at Edinburgh prior to the American Revolution, was a signatory to the Declaration of Independence. Another signatory was John Witherspoon, who had studied theology at Edinburgh before becoming President of the College of New Jersey (Princeton). Two other Edinburgh graduates were instrumental in founding the first two medical schools in America (Philadelphia in 1765 and New York in 1767). Rush also founded the first American anti-slavery society, and his association with Edinburgh possibly led to the University being looked on favourably by students from Africa. James Africanus Beale Horton was the first African to graduate from Edinburgh, receiving his MD degree in 1859.

Eight women graduated in 1893; one is missing from this photograph as she was working abroad by the time of the graduation ceremony.

Born in Sierra Leone and the child of freed slaves, Horton took the name Africanus in recognition of his roots, and left a large part of his estate for the development of scientific education in Africa.

Students came in particular from the countries of the Commonwealth, and by 1875 the number of students coming from India was such that the first ever South Asian student society to be established in the UK was set up at Edinburgh. Pioneers of a different kind were the first women to enrol at the University. The debate about whether or not to admit women to study had raged for many years – not only at Edinburgh, of course – and an association had been established in Edinburgh in 1867 to provide university-level education to women. This enabled a small group of women to graduate in 1893, having undertaken most of their higher education through the association, with just a year spent at the University itself.

Julius Kambarage Nyerere graduated MA in 1952, later returning to receive an honorary degree.

Sophia Jex-Blake was one of seven woman who began studying medicine at Edinburgh in 1869. She was forced to take her degree in Switzerland.

A statue of Dr Huang Kuan, the first Chinese student to graduate from a Western university, stands in the grounds of the Confucius Institute for Scotland in the University of Edinburgh. The health pioneer graduated from Edinburgh's medical school in 1855.

...and from Edinburgh to the world – and beyond

Piers Sellers graduated with his BSc in 1976. © NASA

Many of the early students at the University were studying divinity or medicine, and large numbers of Edinburgh graduates spent their careers abroad as missionaries or doctors.

Others have had a major international influence through their work, such as Robert Louis Stevenson, Charles Darwin, James Clerk Maxwell and David Hume. In modern times, research has become increasingly interdisciplinary and international, and so a research team may comprise partner universities – staff and research students – in several countries. The results of research are increasingly utilised on a global scale, so while, for example, the Centre for Regenerative Medicine is based at the University's site at Little France, the research carried out there influences treatment of chronic conditions around the world. Many students studying at Edinburgh take advantage of the numerous international exchange opportunities available during their studies, in some cases leading to postgraduate-level study abroad.

Edinburgh's graduates have often travelled across the world, but one of our graduates took matters even further. The late Piers Sellers became an astronaut, taking part in space missions. He supported the University in many ways, making a particular contribution in community engagement and outreach. He also unwittingly provided Sir Timothy O'Shea with material for his graduation speeches. Prior to one of his space missions, Piers Sellers suggested to the Principal that he might take the University's graduation 'bunnet' into space. While the Principal thought this was an inspired idea, University administrators did not. A compromise was reached, whereby a small embroidered University logo was taken into space by Piers, and was stitched into the bunnet on his safe return to earth. As Sir Timothy says, this makes the University of Edinburgh unique in conferring the award of degrees by a tap on the head from a medieval fusion space bunnet.

Robert Louis Stevenson.

Charles Darwin began his studies in medicine in 1825 but turned his attentions to biology, leaving in 1827 without graduating.

Eric Liddell, 1924 Olympic medallist.

Gordon Brown, 1970, Prime Minister of the UK 2007-2010.

Piers Sellers, seen here with the graduation 'bunnet'.

The modern graduation ceremony

The graduation ceremony commences when the academic procession walks through the hall to take their places on the platform.

This is a colourful affair with a wonderful mixture of gowns. There are two things that determine which gowns people wear. One of these is the place they graduated from and degree they graduated with – each university has its own colours and designs and students become entitled to wear a particular gown when they graduate. Most members of the academic procession will therefore be wearing gowns specific to their own university and degree. Some people will be wearing gowns associated with a particular role in the University of Edinburgh – the Vice-Chancellor, members of the University Court, and so on.

So who is on the platform at graduation? First to enter are the academics who have been teaching the cohort of graduands and those supervising graduating PhD students. These staff are often members of Senate – the academic governing body of the University. There are also members of the senior administration of the University. Along with them will be members of Court – the largely external independent group which oversees governance of the University. There are office bearers from the Students' Association and also from the General Council – the body which comprises all alumni.

There will be those who are to read the names of the graduating students – usually the heads of the schools of the graduating class. There may be someone about to receive an honorary degree, and a 'laureator' to present them. Someone – often the University Chaplain – will give a moment of reflection to begin the ceremony.

Seen here at a special event in Old College, the Chancellor's robes are embroidered with gold thread; the Vice-Chancellor's with silver.

There may be visiting key people like the Lord Provost of the City. There may be regents of the University – people who devote extensive amounts of time sharing their expertise and experience to help the University in a variety of ways. The last members of the procession to take their places on the platform are the Bedellus or mace bearer and the Vice-Chancellor.

The Vice-Chancellor's robe is embroidered with silver and is very heavy. Standing throughout a whole ceremony in such a robe, constantly raising one's arm to confer degrees on graduands, is a tiring business. The Chancellor sometimes attends graduation; her robes are similar to the Vice-Chancellor's, but are embroidered with gold rather than silver. The Bedellus has a key role in the ceremony, ushering the honorary graduands to their places and ensuring that the ceremony runs smoothly.

The mace the Bedellus carries is not the original one owned by the University. Maces have long been important symbols of authority and were originally carried as protection in the event of trouble from the crowds. When the Tounis College was first established, a silver mace was therefore an early and important acquisition. However, while the fledgling University had a mace, the town council did not, and so on important ceremonial occasions, the town council borrowed the mace from the Tounis College. Council minutes record the loan and return of the University's mace for two hundred years, until one day in 1787 the minutes record that the mace has been stolen. It was never recovered, and in 1789 the current mace was donated by the town council as a replacement.

The Bedellus, Keith Black, leading the Vice-Chancellor to the platform.

Captain Elder, Bedellus and Mace-bearer for 26 years, is seen here just prior to his retirement in 1972, with the then Chancellor, the Duke of Edinburgh.

Veterinary Medicine graduands preparing for their class photo outside the Usher Hall in 2016.

Names are double-checked against lists before graduands go up to the platform.

The Chancellor capping a graduand at a ceremony in the Usher Hall, 2016.

Students unveil the University's tartan.

The hat or 'bunnet' with which the Vice-Chancellor confers degrees is also part of tradition, as explained by Sir Timothy in the speech he makes at each ceremony, standing at the front of the platform with the academic staff members seated behind him:

"Those watching from far and near may be wondering why I have spent the last hour hitting our graduates on the head with this hat. This is a peculiar tradition in Scottish universities, adapted from the practices of slavery in the ancient world. I have been manumitting our graduates, freeing them from the bondage imposed on them by this lot behind me [referring to the academic staff seated behind him on the platform]. As our degree titles suggest, you, our graduates, have now become Masters of your subjects, you are no longer in a state of subjection. A 17th century history of the University tells us all this was once accompanied by very stern and very long exhortations that you should henceforth lead virtuous lives. I will spare you that today and restrict myself to celebrating your mastery of the subjects taught."

As was the case with all the European universities, Edinburgh was founded primarily as an institution to train men for the church, and so it is no surprise that the early laureation and graduation ceremonies contained prayers and possibly a sermon, and aspects of that tradition continued until very recently. Increasing numbers of international students made it important to offer a ceremony which would include everyone, regardless of faith – as the University Chaplaincy describes itself, a place 'for people of all faiths and none' – and so a member of staff or a member of the University Court or the General Council now delivers a 'moment of reflection' rather than a prayer at the start of the ceremony.

The dress code for graduands has always specified formal dress in black and white, but national dress has also been permitted – and indeed, encouraged. Kilts have become more popular in recent years, and as many international students were also keen to wear kilts, the University had its own tartan designed and registered. Woven predominantly in the blue and red of the University crest, it has become a popular choice with graduands with no clan affiliation. Edinburgh is unusual in not having any sort of hat or mortar board as part of its graduation dress, and the one exception which is made is for head-coverings which are required as part of a graduand's religious observance.

Graduands applauding their colleagues

Music in ceremonies

The organ

The Graduation Choir with their director, Dr John Kitchen, University and City organist

The organ

The organ was not part of Anderson's original design; its installation was something of an afterthought.

Although organs are generally associated with churches, the Victorians were keen to have organs in public halls, and the organ in the McEwan Hall has always played an important part in graduation ceremonies.

Robert Hope-Jones, an eccentric but innovative builder, was given the contract to install the organ, which has over 4,000 pipes. The layout he used is odd, due to the fact that no provision had been made for an organ in the original plans, but the resonant acoustic of the hall makes it a success.

We have little information about the organ's use in graduations in the early 20th century, although there are a few articles about the instrument itself in specialist periodicals. Herrick Bunney found the organ very unreliable when he took over as University Organist in the late 1940s, and sadly in need of repair. Dr Bunney also noted that graduations in those days were rowdy affairs, and recalled a plucked chicken being thrown through the air and narrowly missing him.

At Herrick Bunney's instigation, the organ was completely remodelled by Henry Willis III in 1953, and continued to be much used, not just for graduations, but for recitals. Dr John Kitchen took over as University Organist in 1989, and has played at almost every graduation ceremony since. The organ was again comprehensively rebuilt in 2013–14 and should now be in very good shape for the next 50 years or more. Its majestic sound greatly enhances graduation ceremonies.

The graduation choir

By contrast with the organ, the Graduation Choir is a relatively recent development, instigated by Sir Timothy O'Shea.

At his request, Dr Kitchen was happy to set up a small choir to sing at each ceremony. The ceremonies had previously been performed with appropriate style and dignity, but around this time some changes were being considered to make them more engaging and varied. The Principal felt that a short musical interlude would add to this. Choral interludes had featured occasionally prior to this – for example, when the composer Sir James MacMillan was awarded an honorary degree, some of his music was performed during the ceremony. But it was a new idea to have a choir at every ceremony. A group of around 12 to 15 singers – numbers vary from ceremony to ceremony, depending on who is available – form the Graduation Choir and their contribution to the ceremonies has proved highly popular.

Two songs are usually sung during the ceremony, from a varied repertoire. Arrangements of Scottish songs, particularly to poems by Robert Burns, usually feature; 'The Birks of Aberfeldy' is a firm favourite. The choir also sings folk songs of other countries as well as madrigals, British part songs by composers such as Elgar, Parry and Stanford, and sometimes jazz classics such as Gershwin's 'I got rhythm'. Occasionally the traditional university graduation song, 'Gaudeamus igitur', makes an outing too.

University of Edinburgh hood designs

Undergraduate awards

Undergraduate hoods © Ede & Ravenscroft 2017

Postgraduate awards

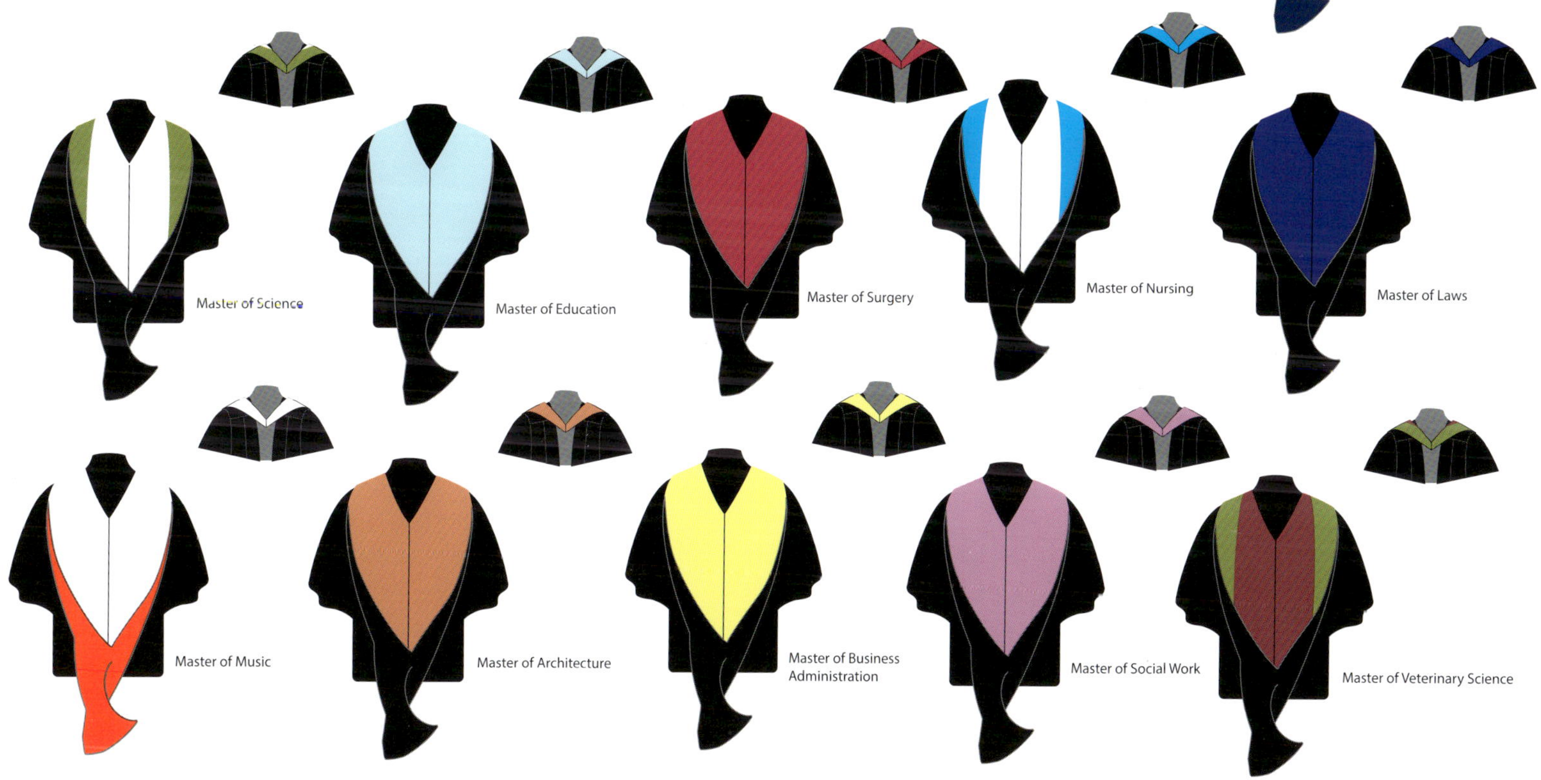

Postgraduate hoods © Ede & Ravenscroft 2017

Recognising lifetime achievements

As mentioned above, the University awarded an honorary degree to William McEwan in gratitude for his generosity to the institution.

This would not be done in modern times; honorary degrees are now awarded solely in recognition of the achievements of people in their chosen fields. Were Mr McEwan around today, he would instead be recognised as a University Benefactor, as a number of individuals or organisations have been. To separate out the giving of honorary degrees for excellence from recognising those who support the University in other ways, a new award of University Benefactor was developed in 2008. This is presented to partnerships, companies, charities or individuals who have helped the University in some substantial way – either financially or through a donation such as a library or collection of manuscripts or paintings, or through a long standing personal commitment such as involvement in fundraising activities or general support to the University. Those receiving the awards are generally exceptional people themselves, being very senior in a trust or organisation, or having earned large sums of money for their entrepreneurial endeavours, for example.

The first academic staff of the Tounis College were titled 'regents' and a single regent was responsible for guiding his students throughout their four years of study. The title has been re-used recently in a different context. Modern regents are the way that the University recognises and harnesses the knowledge, expertise and guidance of a nominated group of volunteers.

Neil Armstrong, astronaut with the Vice-Chancellor.

Each regent has a specific and tailored role that reflects the skills of the individual and the requirements of the projects in which they choose to be involved. Regents advise on key project areas including philanthropy, alumni engagement, working with University of Edinburgh Trusts and governing bodies, international student recruitment and public engagement. When the University decided to reintroduce the title, a competition was held in Edinburgh College of Art to design an appropriate gown for regents to wear at ceremonies, and the successful student then worked with the University's robe-makers, Ede & Ravenscroft, to bring the design to fruition.

Another recent innovation is the introduction by the Principal of two new awards for staff or students. The Exceptional Service Award recognises staff members or teams who have delivered exceptional service by devoting time and energy beyond what is expected of their position to supporting and serving the University community and mission, while the Contribution to the Community Award honours staff members or students, as individuals or groups, who have played a key role in a project with the community they have worked in, lived in or contributed to.

Katherine Grainger returned to Edinburgh to name a new boat for the rowing club.

Honorary degrees are awarded at each ceremony to individuals who have excelled in their professional fields. For those who are famous faces – like sports stars or musicians – they need to have excelled in their field and be contributing to the wider community through their activities, for example by supporting and encouraging young people, or being a leader in charitable work.

Dame Stella Rimington, former Director General of MI5.

Each College has the opportunity to nominate possible recipients, and a final selection is made by a committee which makes recommendations to the University's Senate. Awards are made at the most relevant ceremony – so at the ceremony at which students in engineering graduate, for example, the recipient of the honorary degree is likely to be an engineer or someone who has made a major contribution in a related field. Honorary degrees – with the exception of the degree of Doctor *honoris causa* – cannot be awarded to current members of staff of the University of Edinburgh.

While many honorary graduates are academics, others have excelled in business, sports, or the performing arts. The violinist Nicola Benedetti was awarded the degree of Doctor of Music in 2011, rower and sports ambassador Katherine Grainger was awarded the degree of Doctor *honoris causa* in the same year, and The Reverend Jesse Louis Jackson, Sr., civil rights activist, was awarded the degree of Doctor *honoris causa* in 2015. Julius Kambarage Nyerere, formerly Prime Minister of Tanganyika, was awarded the degree of Doctor of Laws in 1962. Poet Sorley MacLean was awarded the degree of Doctor of Letters in 1980, and Professor Emeritus Peter Higgs was awarded the Doctor of Science in 1998 for his work in theoretical physics; in 2013 scientists at CERN confirmed the existence of the Higgs particle. As just a few examples from the hundreds of people who have been recognised in this way over the centuries, these honorary graduates demonstrate the breadth of human knowledge and achievement.

Archbishop Desmond Tutu receiving his honorary degree.

Violinist Nicola Benedetti received an honorary degree in 2011.

King Olav of Norway received the honorary degree of Doctor of Laws in October 1962.

President of Ireland, Michael D Higgins.

His Serene Highness Prince Albert II of Monaco.

Michael Palin, actor and author.

Some notable graduates over the centuries

The students graduating today join an impressive roll call of alumni of the University of Edinburgh.

So many of our alumni have gone on to make major contributions in their fields that it is difficult to select just a few – and of course, as the early students did not necessarily 'graduate' as such, not all of those shown here hold degrees from Edinburgh. For every one of the people listed we could have named a dozen others, so these are just a few examples of the ways in which alumni and former students have contributed in past centuries.

ERIC LIDDELL
1924
Olympic medallist

HASTINGS BANDA
1941
President of Malawi

JOHN WITHERSPOON
1739
Signatory to the American Declaration of Independence

JOHN CRAWFURD
1803
Second Resident (Governor) of Singapore

ROBERT ADAM
Architect

PETER MARK ROGET
1798
Developed his Thesaurus of English Words and Phrases

CHRYSTAL MACMILLAN
1896
First woman to graduate in science, later retrained in law

CHARLOTTE AUERBACH
1935
Animal Geneticist (1935)

DAVID BREWSTER
1800
Researcher in optics, inventor of the kaleidoscope, and Principal of the University of Edinburgh from 1859

GORDON BROWN
1970
Prime Minister of the UK 2007-2010

ADD YOUR OWN FAVOURITE HERE

BENJAMIN RUSH
1768
Signatory to the American Declaration of Independence

GRACE FAIRLEY
1893

YON POSUN
1929
President of South Korea

ADAM FERGUSON
1742
Key figure in the Scottish Enlightenment and the father of modern sociology

JULIUS KAMBARAGE NYERERE
1952
First President of Tanzania

SOPHIA JEX-BLAKE
Physician and pioneer of medical education for women

ROBIN COOK
1968
Politician

CHARLES DARWIN
Naturalist

ROBERT LOUIS STEVENSON
Author

DAVID STEEL
1960
Politician

JAMES CLERK MAXWELL
Mathematician and scientist

PIERS SELLERS
1976
Astronaut

ROBERT LORIMER
Architect

MALCOLM RIFKIND
1966
Politician

JAMES YOUNG SIMPSON
1832
Pioneer of anaesthesia

SALLY MAGNUSSON
1982
Broadcaster and writer

KATHERINE GRAINGER
1997
Olympic medallist

IAN RANKIN
1982
Author

WALTER SCOTT
Novelist

PHILIPPA GREGORY
1985
Author

STELLA RIMINGTON
1958
Director-General of MI5

ADD YOUR OWN FAVOURITE HERE

ALEXANDER MCCALL SMITH
1971
Author

ADD YOUR OWN FAVOURITE HERE

ROBERT ROWAND ANDERSON
Architect

ELIZABETH BLACKADDER
1970
Artist

CHRIS HOY
1999
Olympic medallist

Behind the scenes

The Principal, Sir Timothy O'Shea.

The University usually runs seventeen ceremonies in the summer and another nine in November.

Approximately 8,000 students graduate each year. A huge amount of work goes on behind the scenes to enable this all to happen. Like a blockbuster film, the list of credits could run for several minutes if everyone who had contributed in some way was listed. Staff in Academic Services (previously called the Registry) have spent weeks preparing for the ceremonies. Staff in Schools have marked exams and essays, checking and re-checking exam board minutes and lists of marks – and in a few cases, an academic appeal will have been considered. Programmes have been prepared, degree certificates have been printed, tickets have been issued, last minute changes of mind as to whether a student is attending in person or graduating in absentia have been accommodated. Gowns have been ordered, sorted and hung up ready for collection.

The Servitors carry out ceremonial duties, including assisting at graduations.

The academic staff presenting students for graduation will have gone through the lists of names, checking the pronunciation of any they are not sure of – a major feat when so many students are from abroad.

On the day itself, the servitors have a key role in getting the graduates all in the right seats in the right order, sending them up to the platform at the right time, and coping with any unexpected hitches. Other staff are on hand to show families to their seats, to issue graduation programmes, or to tidy up afterwards. Many Schools host receptions for the new graduates and their families. All these preparations are key to graduation being a lovely and memorable event – not just for those attending in person, but for the increasing number of family and friends overseas who watch the ceremony live online.

A lot of work goes on behind the scenes to ensure all graduands are in the right place at the right time.

Servitors enjoy the ceremony too.

TV presenter Sally Magnusson makes a regular appearance at the Edinburgh International Book Festival where she interviews the judges for the James Tait Black Awards before presenting the prizes to the authors.

Life after graduation

The graduates crossing the platform today are following a tradition stretching back for over 400 years.

Some of them will embark on their professional lives as alumni of the University of Edinburgh with barely a backward glance, while others will keep their connections with their alma mater – or may rediscover those connections some years after graduating. Alumni take responsibility for running alumni clubs in many parts of the world, offering graduates the opportunity to meet with others sharing the common thread of time spent at Edinburgh. Many alumni use their professional lives to keep their links with Edinburgh strong – and of course, some go on to careers within the University itself.

Alumni automatically become members of the General Council of the University of Edinburgh. The General Council consists of graduates, academic staff and members of the supreme governing body of the University, the University Court. It has a statutory right to comment on matters which affect the wellbeing and prosperity of the University, with the aim of ensuring that graduates have a continuing voice in the management of the University's affairs. The General Council elects the University's Chancellor, three Assessors to the University Court and its own Business Committee. It also has the responsibility of maintaining a register of all University of Edinburgh graduates.

The General Council meets on a regular basis – and has done since it was formed in 1858 – and meetings now take place not just in Edinburgh but abroad. The Development and Alumni team at the University is happy to assist alumni in keeping in touch.

The University is always pleased to hear about the progress of a student and proud when they are successful and contribute to the wider community. Our community of staff and students, past and present, *is* the University of Edinburgh.

Alumni clubs around the world organise events, such as this Burns Supper in Toronto.

About the authors

Jean Grier (left) and Mary Bownes have both spent significant parts of their careers at the University of Edinburgh. With over 30 years in a wide range of administrative posts at the University, Jean has developed a particular interest in the history of the University and the city. Prior to her recent retirement after 37 years at the University of Edinburgh, Mary (seen here in her role as Acting Vice-Chancellor) was a professor of developmental biology while also serving as a Vice-Principal from 2003 and as Senior Vice-Principal from 2012. *Graduation: Celebrating 400 Years of Personal Achievement* is the third book Jean and Mary have co-authored about the University. Their other books are *Private Giving, Public Good: The Impact of Philanthropy at the University of Edinburgh* and *Digging up our Past: The Archaeological Excavations in Old College Quad.*

Acknowledgments

Like the graduation ceremony itself, pulling a book together requires the enthusiasm and cooperation of many people, and many colleagues have contributed facts and figures, anecdotes, or directions to possible sources of information.

The majority of the illustrations used in this book have come from University sources or from material owned by the authors. We are grateful in particular to the Centre for Research Collections for a number of the historical images and to Communications and Marketing for the majority of the photographs. Douglas Robertson was the photographer for many of the graduation photographs and pictures of the McEwan Hall. Other photographers include Ross Gillespie, Tricia Malley and Gordon Robertson. LDN Architects kindly gave permission to use some of their site illustrations and photographs taken during the redevelopment of the McEwan Hall. John Cormack of Ede & Ravenscroft produced the graphic summary of the different hoods in use at Edinburgh.

Every effort has been made to trace copyright holders, but if any have been inadvertently overlooked, the publisher will be pleased to make the necessary arrangement at the first opportunity.

Our thanks also go to many colleagues including Keith Black, Grant Buttars, Crawford Ferguson, Jane Herkes, Sheena Jenkins, John Kitchen, Drew Laven, Robert Lawrie, Susan Pettigrew and Lizzie Robinson, and alumni Simon Miles and Ian McGregor.

ROYAUME-UNI
NORD-PAS-DE-CALAIS
BELGIQUE
ALLEMAGNE
LUXEMBOURG
GUADELOUPE
HAUTE-NORMANDIE
PICARDIE
BASSE-NORMANDIE
ILE-DE-FRANCE
CHAMPAGNE-ARDENNE
LORRAINE
ALSACE
MARTINIQUE
BRETAGNE
PAYS-DE-LA-LOIRE
CENTRE
BOURGOGNE
FRANCHE-COMTÉ
SUISSE
GUYANE
POITOU-CHARENTES
LIMOUSIN
RHÔNE-ALPES
ITALIE
AUVERGNE
AQUITAINE
MIDI-PYRÉNÉES
PROVENCE-ALPES-CÔTE D'AZUR
LANGUEDOC-ROUSSILLON
CORSE
RÉUNION
ESPAGNE

Summary

Physical France

Vineyards and Appellations

ALSACE

Gewürztraminer
Riesling
Pinot gris
Muscat
Pinot
Sylvaner
Pinot noir
Grand cru

BEAUJOLAIS

1. St-Amour
2. Juliénas
3. Chénas
4. Moulin-à-Vent
5. Fleurie
6. Chiroubles
7. Morgon
8. Regnié
9. Côte-de-Brouilly
10. Brouilly

BORDELAIS

1. St-Estèphe
2. Pauillac
3. St-Julien
4. Listrac
5. Moulis
6. Margaux
7. Haut-Médoc
8. Pessac-Léognan
9. Graves
10. Cérons
11. Barsac
12. Sauternes
13. Loupiac
14. Ste-Croix-du-Mont
15. Pomerol
16. Lalande de Pomerol
17. St-Émilion

BOURGOGNE

1. Gevrey-Chambertin
2. Chambolle-Musigny
3. Vougeot
4. Vosne-Romanée
5. Nuits-St-Georges
6. Aloxe-Corbon
7. Beaune
8. Pommard
9. Volnay
10. Meursault
11. Puligny-Montrachet
12. Rully
13. Mercurey
14. Chassagne-Montrachet

JURA

1. Arbois
2. Château-Châlon
3. L'Étoile
4. Côtes-du-Jura

LANGUEDOC

1. Coteaux du Languedoc
2. Faugères
3. Limoux
4. Cabardès
5. Côtes de la Malepère
6. Fitou

SAVOIE

1. Abymes
2. Apremont
3. Ripaille
4. Chignin
5. Crépy
6. Seyssel

SUD-OUEST

1. Buzet
2. Côtes-du-Brulhois
3. Vin de Lavilledieu
4. Côtes-du-Frontonnais
5. Tursan
6. Côtes de St-Mont
7. Pacherenc-du-Vic-Bilh

VALLÉE DE LA LOIRE

1. Savennières
2. Chaume
3. Bonnezeaux
4. Quarts de Chaume
5. Coteaux-de-l'Aubance
6. Bourgueil
7. St-Nicolas-de-Bourgueil
8. Chinon
9. Cheverny
10. Valencay
11. Menetou-Salon
12. Quincy
13. Reuilly
14. Châteaumeillant
15. St-Pourçain
16. Côte Roannaise
17. Côte d'Auvergne
18. Cotes du Forez

VALLÉE DU RHÔNE

1. Condrieu
2. Château-Grillet
3. Côte-Rotie
4. St-Joseph
5. Cornas
6. St-Péray
7. Crozes-Hermitage
8. Hermitage
9. Beaumes-de-Venise
10. Gigondas
11. Châteauneuf-du-Pape
12. Lirac
13. Tavel

*The **Carnac** Alignments (megalithic). (Morbihan.)*

*Rupestrine paintings in the **Font-de-Gaume** grotto (10,000 - 15,000 B.C). (Dordogne.)*

History and Architecture

35000-10000
The appearance of Homo sapiens. The **Dordogne and Vézère valleys**: rock paintings.

4500-2000
Megalithic civilisation starts to appear in **Brittany**, and **Corsica.**

59-51 B.C.
Gaul, then inhabited by people of Celtic and Iberian origin, is conquered by Julius Cesar. Monuments of great architectural interest have been left by this Gallo-Roman civilisation. During the 3rd century barbarian invasions devastated the country.

481-511
Clovis, King of the Francs was baptised, in 498, at **Reims**.

800
The coronation of Charlemagne, who established a huge western empire. This empire was divided up into three parts by the treaty of Verdun in 843. Western Francie, to the west of the Escaut, Meuse and Rhône rivers, becoming France.

987
Hugues Capet ascends the throne of France.

*The Château Comt… **Carcassonne**, a je… of medieval militar… architecture. (Aude…*

*The " Maison Carrée " at **Nîmes**, Roman temple built during the reign of Auguste. (Gard.)*

The chapter of the **Abbey at Fontenay***: asceticism, work and spirituality, the very principles of the monastic life. (Côte-d'Or.)*

From the 11th century to the middle of the 12th century

Central power weakness results in a feudal system: local nobility construct fortified castles. The revival of the Christian faith is manifested by the spread of churches, monasteries, and priories. Simplicity of shape, and harmony of space, animated by sculpture which was both innovative and controlled, characterising Roman art.

Middle of the 12th–13th century

Population growth, the development of cities, the enhancement of land, along with the thirst for knowledge raises medieval civilisation to its peak. During this time of enrichment daring cathedrals arose from the ground, particularly in the Greater Paris Area. The use of intersecting ribs in construction reduced the supporting role of walls: masses of light now penetrating through huge stained glass windows.

1337–1475

The One Hundred Years War, within an environment of misery and troubles has the Capetians attempting to repulse the English. Du Guesclin re-establishes order, and in 1429 Joan of Arc liberates Orléans. The treaty of Picquigny (1475), signed by Louis XI, puts an end to hostilities.

Vézelay*: chapiter of the mystical Mill, an alliance of movement and ease of flow, beginning of the 12th century. (Yonne.)*

Rouen *Cathedral nave and choir, an audacious masterpiece of Middle Age period building. (Seine-Maritime.)*

16th century

Despite the religious crisis of the Reformation, a wind of renewal blows throughout France: the Renaissance results in the flowering of humanism, and a refined art of living, symbolised by the châteaux of the Loire.

Azay-le-Rideau, *one of the most elegant of the Loire chateaux, built between 1518 and 1527. (Indre-et-Loire.)*

The Château at **Versailles***: a symbol of the absolute power of royalty during the time of Louis 14th. (Yvelines.)*

Cathedra of the **Church of Conflans-Albertville***: the exuberance of baroque sculpture. (Savoie.)*

1643-1715

The reign of Louis XIV, the "Sun King", is a period of military success (France is the major European power), literature (Molière, Racine, Boileau, La Fontaine) and the arts (Mansart, Le Brun). The Château de Versailles reflecting the triumph of absolutism as a synthesis of national resources around an absolute monarchy. This classical architecture (methodical distribution of mass), the expression of controlled passion, is succeeded by baroque which loosens the rules (spanning of volumes, the liberation of symmetry, curves, sculpture). The end of the 18th century is marked by a return to academicism: neo-classical architecture combining new techniques to the magnificence of Greek and Roman antiquity.

1789-1793

An extended political, social, and financial crisis puts an end to the "Ancien Régime". Louis XVI is beheaded on January 21, 1793.

1804-1815

Napoléon is crowned emperor of the French in **Paris**, and perfects France's administrative organisation. But wars with European countries resulting in the abdication at Fontainebleau, and the Waterloo defeat, weaken the country.

1815-1848

After the restoration of the monarchy (Louis XVIII and Charles X), Louis-Philippe establishes a constitutional monarchy prior to being overthrown in February 1848.

The neo-classical facade, so called "Louis 16th " of the **Château at Valençay***. (Indre.)*

The Viaduc at Garabit, *built between 1882 and 1884 by Gustave Eiffel, has a central span of 116 meters. (Cantal.)*

The **Orsay Railway Station**, *converted into a museum, built at the end of the 19th century: new techniques enabled increasingly vast buildings to be raised. (Paris.)*

1848-1870

The Second Republic in 1851 gives way to the Second Empire. The reign of Napoleon III was noted for an expansion of the industrial revolution which was made possible by the development of mechanisation and the use of coal and iron. The disastrous war against Prussia resulted in 1871 in the loss of Alsace, and a part of Lorraine.

1871-1939

The Third Republic introduced considerable reforms: free and compulsory primary education, trade union legalisation, the separation of Church and State. Foreign policy was oriented towards colonial expansion. The Great War (1914-1918) finished with victory over Germany, but left France worn out. New needs (large department stores, railway stations, exhibition halls) along with revolutionary structures (metal frame structures) gave birth to an architecture oriented towards the liberation of useful surface space, and increasingly larger areas.

1939-1945

The Second World War.

1945 UNTIL TODAY

Modernisation of the country, and European construction are the priorities of the Fourth and Fifth Republics. The use of new materials (concrete, aluminium, glass) increases the creativeness of architects.

The François Mitterrand "Bibliothèque de France": *the use of new materials permits the most daring of shapes. (Paris.)*

Alsace

The Alsace region covers of the western slopes of the Vosges and the Rhineland plain which extends from Sundgau in the south to the German border in the north. On the lower slopes of the Vosges thrive the vineyards which for the most part produce the famous Riesling, Sylvaner, and Gewurztraminer white wines. The plain, or ried as it is known, is the area of orchards and grassland. Very picturesque floral villages (Ribeauvillé, Riquewihr, Kayersberg...), consisting of beamed houses are, at times, overlooked by fortified castles.

Strasbourg, Headquarters of the Council of Europe and the European Parliament continues to assert its European prominence at an artistic, intellectual, and political level. Its cathedral, the building of which commenced in 1176, is in pink sandstone from the Vosges, and has a superb radiating facade.

Colmar, at the heart of the Alsace plain, based its prosperity on the wine trade as from the 13th century. The old city charms by its beamed residences, and numerous canals evocative of a "Small Venice".

The area of **"Petite France" at Strasbourg** *is the old tanning and milling quarter. Its houses dating from the Renaissance line the branches of the River Ill. (Bas-Rhin.)*

The red sandstone houses of Riquewihr *form an homogeneous village in the middle of an Alsace vineyard. (Haut-Rhin.)*

The Haut-Koenigsbourg château *dominates the plain of Alsace. Its ruins were re-erected at the start of the 20th century by Emperor William II. (Vosges.)*

Further to the south is the lively city of **Mulhouse,** heir to a powerful industrial tradition of which several museums give witness: the National Automobile Museum (the Schlumpf collection), the French Railway Museum, Electropolis, The Printed Fabrics' Museum, and the Wallpaper Museum.

The Roman church at Murbach, *near Mulhouse, has retained its flat chevet overlooked by the high towers of the transept. (Haut-Rhin.)*

The Retable at Buhl *(about 1500) was painted, probably, for Saint Catherine's convent at Colmar. It depicts scenes from the Passion of Christ. (Haut-Rhin.)*

Aequitaine

The Aequitaine region which combines the Périgord, the Bordeaux region, the Landes area, the Basque Country, and the west of the Pyrenean chain, contains a huge variety of countryside. The Périgord, area, one of the cradles of humanity with its numerous upper Paleolithic (35000 to 10000 B.C) decorated grottoes, is renowned for its conserves, foie gras, and the truffles which form beneath the oak and hazelnut trees which make up the magnificent forests. **Sarlat-la-Canéda**, the capital of Périgord Noir, is proud of its beautiful residences, which date from the 13th century, and were raised by wealthy traders, the middle classes, and magistrates. The Saint-Front cathedral, at **Périgueux**, is the most beautiful example of a Périgord domed church.

The mellow reliefs of the "Pays de Cize", *in the Basque country, bear the stamp of the work of man. (Pyrénées-Atlantiques.)*

The Bordeaux area is universally known for the quality of its vineyards which run along the banks of the Garonne and Gironde rivers. Trade in their produce was for a long time responsible for the prosperity of Bordeaux, first ranking port in the Kingdom during the 15th century, the period during which the Place de la Bourse and the Place du Parlement were built. The Landes' region is one huge forest of pines planted during the last century, on one side bordered by the Atlantic, the surfers paradise. To the south lies the Basque Country a region of noted character which has its own culture, and language. The coast with its ragged cliffs and fine beaches is overlooked by green valleys dotted with white houses, this is the area of Labourd. **Biarritz** is an old fishing port which was transformed during the last century into a seaside resort. The other major resort, **Saint-Jean-de-Luz**, has retained its fishing port which concentrates on sardines, tuna, and anchovies. The ancient provinces of Lower Navarre and Soule present a rugged relief, covered with vast forests of pine and beech. **Pau**, birthplace of Henri IV offers a superb view of the Pyrenees.

Atlantic rains feed the rich **grassland of the Basque country,** *a region devoted to pastoral activity. (Pyrénées-Atlantiques.)*

The church at Oloron-Sainte-Marie *has a Roman portal the arches of which depict the Aged of the Apocalypse, some of them playing music. (Pyrénées-Atlantiques.)*

Old Bordeaux *is one of the most beautiful examples of 18th century town planning. The " Place de la Bourse ", designed by the father and son architects, Gabriel, gives witness to the wealth of the city, at that time first ranking port in the Kingdom. (Gironde.)*

The Vineyards of Bordeaux *cover more than 130,000 hectares. Approximately eight thousand "châteaux" produce vintage wines the names of which are a veritable list of fame: Saint-Estèphe, Margaux, Pauillac, Château-Yquem, Saint-Emilion... (Gironde.)* Ph. R. Nourry

The Landes' Forest *was first planted in the 19th century. It consists of maritime pines, a fast growing rectilinear tree. (Landes.)*

The large beach *at Saint-Jean-de-Luz, between the Pyrenees and the Atlantic Ocean. (Pyrénées-Atlantiques.)*

Bayonne, between "les Landes" and the Basque country, *is the economic centre of the Adour region. The banks of the River Nive are lined with big picturesque houses. (Pyrénées-Atlantiques.)*

The Roque-Gageac *is considered to be the most beautiful site in the Dordogne valley. Its houses with roofs or flag stones and tiles are bunched together at the bottom of the cliff. (Dordogne.)*

Périgueux *was for a long time shared between the City, once part of ancient Vésone, and the powerful monastic centre of Puy-Saint-Front which attracted a multitude of pilgrims. (Dordogne.)*

The Walled town of Monpazier, *founded by Edward 1st, Duke of Aquitaine and King of England, was part of the system of defence established in the Périgord as from 1267. (Dordogne.)*

The Fortress at Bonaguil *(15th-16th centuries) is a fine example of architecture which integrated firearms within its defensive system. (Lot-et-Garonne.)*

Auvergne

The volcanic massifs of the Auvergne form the backbone of the Massif Central which covers a major part of the region. From the south to the north, the Cantal (highest point being the Plomb du Cantal 1,858 meters) the heights of Dore (Puy de Sancy, 1,886 meters) and Dome (Puy de Dome, 1,463 meters) - puy signifying mountain in auvergnat- make for original scenery consisting of cones, more or less eroded, and lakes the result of certain valleys being closed by the flow of lava; On the slopes forests and pasture alternate, and provide grazing for the tough tan coated salers cattle. Numerous

The Sancy volcanic massif *is a paradise for strolling enthusiasts; its numerous paths criss-cross a preserved environment. (Puy-de-Dôme.)*

mineral and hot water springs have resulted in the founding of a considerable number of medical treatment spas. To the east of these volcanoes the Bourbonnais mountains, the Forez and Livradois, alternate with pasture and forests.

At the foot of the Puy-de-Dôme lies **Clermont-Ferrand** which is partially built from stone formed from lava. Since the end of the last century it has become the city of the tyre, and Headquarters of the Michelin company. Moulins, the Bourbonnais capital has numerous agricultural connected activities: food produce, foot wear .... Aurillac, at the centre of Upper Auvergne has retained and old area of winding narrow streets which descend to the Jordanne river. The Puy-en-Velay occupies an original location in a huge basin bristling with volcanic needles, on one of these the cathedral of Notre-Dame has been raised .

Thiers *has, for several centuries now, specialised in cutlery. The Museum of Cutlery: knife with carved ivory handle. (Puy-de-Dôme.)*

The Auvergne Volcano Park, *to the west of Clermont-Ferrand, is a real open air museum of volcanic shapes. (Puy-de-Dôme.)*

The Church of Saint-Nectaire *raised in a verdant environment, is a fine example of Auvergne Roman architecture. Its chevet has an elegant disposition. (Puy-de-Dôme.)*

The Basilica of Saint Julien de Brioude *is the biggest Roman building in the Auvergne area. The warm colouring emanating from the red sandstone and a fine polychrome paving characterise the nave, the first spans of which are supported by grouped pillars of engaged columns. (Haute-Loire.)*

The Cantal *consists of a volcanic relief ground down by glaciers where forest and rich pasture land alternate. (Cantal.)*

The Gorges de la Truyère *crosses the granite plateaux of Upper Auvergne. Some of them have been partially transformed into lakes by dams. (Cantal.)*

Aurillac, *at the crossroads of the Upper Auvergne tourist routes, has retained its old quarter on the banks of the River Jordanne. (Cantal.)*

Burgundy

Beaune, capital of the Burgundy rich patrimony vineyard, *is proud of its general hospital which was founded in 1143 along Flemish lines, for the accommodation of the sick and afflicted. Its roofs are covered with glazed tiles. (Côte-d'Or.)*

Burgundy owes its fame to a rich historical past, the dynasty of the Grand Dukes of Valois (1364-1477), and to the prestigious "Côte" vines which border the "mountain" that dominates the plain of the Saône river. Ancient capital of the Dukes of Burgundy, **Dijon**, since the 15th century became a wealthy city endowed with remarkable monuments: the Dukes' Palace and Burgundy Assembly, the Church of Notre-Dame, and the Hôtel de Vogüe.

To the west the Massif of Morvan retains huge natural open spaces with scattered habitation. The scenery is dominated by forests on the high ground, and hedged pasture land on the slopes. **Nevers**, washed by the Loire river, is famous for its glazed earthenware which was introduced around 1565 by artists of Italian origin. From Auxerre to Dijon stretches the extended Burgundy limestone plateau, which is crossed by numerous rivers and canals which are used for river tourism

Auxerre, the capital of Lower Burgundy, is on the banks of the River Yonne, its old quarter dominated by the Saint-Etienne Cathedral. To the south, hills and undulating plateaux make up the Charollais country, the rich pasture land which is used for raising the reputed beef cattle. The Saône valley, passage way to the south of France, enjoys considerable economic activity which is especially noticeable around **Chalon-sur-Saône**.
The vitality of Roman art is to be seen everywhere; the finest examples being at **Cluny**, **Paray-le-Monial**, **Autun**, **Saulieu** and **Vézelay**.

Cluny Abbey, *founded during the 10th century, is where the extraordinary influence of the Benedictines throughout the Europe of the Middle Ages originated. Very fine capitals originating from the church are exhibited in the flour store. (Saône-et-Loire.)*

Between Chagny and Dijon, to the south of Beaune, the **Burgundian vineyard** *disposes of 37,500 hectares on the slopes which produce the most famous, prestigiously named, vintages in the world: Gevrey-Chambertin, Clos-Vougeot, Vosne-Romanée, Nuits-Saint-Georges, Aloxe-Corton, Pommard. Above: the cellars of the Meursault estate. To the right: grape harvesting on the "Hautes-Côtes de Beaune". (Côte-d'Or.)*

The Fontenay Abbey, *founded in 1118, is built in the architectural tradition of the Cistercians; a visit to the buildings (here the cloister) gives an appreciation of the day in the life of a monk. (Côte-d'Or.)*

The estate of the Clos-Vougeot Château *belongs to the Tastevin (wine tasting) Fraternity who meet each year in chapter to enthrone new members. The order works for the promotion of the wines of both Burgundy and France as a whole. (Côte-d'Or.)*

The Philippe-le-Bon tower which dominates the Dukes' Palace and the Burgundy Assembly, the view takes in the greater part of Dijon. **The Hôtel de Vogüe**, *covered with glazed tiles, adjoins the elegant gothic construction of* **the church of Notre-Dame**. *(Côte-d'Or.)*

The Bussy-Rabutin Château, *an ancient fortress transformed during the 16th century by Antoine de Chandio into a hospitable residence, on his return from Italy, owes its fame to its interior decoration. This was done by Roger de Rabutin, exiled in Burgundy for having sang songs which made light of the relationship of Louis XIV and Marie Mancini, allegorical panels can be admired along with portraits of famous gentlemen and ladies of the court. (Côte-d'Or.)*

Brittany

Brittany firstly brings to mind the coastline "Armor", of which 1,300 kilometres include an infinity of points, coves, and creeks which shelter the fishing ports of **Brest, Lorient**, Le Guilvinec, **Concarneau, Douarnenez**, and **Paimpol**, and a string of isles exposed to the onslaughts of the ocean: Bréhat, Ouessant, Sein, Groix, and Belle-Ile. The interior of the country "Argoat" is partially covered with forests and moors, retaining much evidence of its still living faith in its granite sculpted enclosures and wayside crosses. Agriculture along with the raising of stock occupy a very important place in the local economy: early fruit and vegetables, pork, poultry, and dairy products are exported throughout the entire world.

To the west of Cape Fréhel lies **Erquy** *which is devoted to coastal fishing, mainly for scallops. Its beaches are sheltered from the wind and the ocean swell. (Côtes-d'Armor.)*

The Raz Point *is located at the end of Cape Sizun. It's sombre rocky bulk surrounds, along with Sein island, the very dangerous Raz de Sein with its violent currents and scattering of reefs. (Finistère.)*

Ancient capital of the Duchy of Brittany, then administrative centre of the province when it became part of France as a result of the marriage of Anne de Bretagne to Charles VIII in 1491, **Rennes**, during the last few decades has experienced considerable development in the fields of electronics, telecommunications, and data processing. Its universities have almost 40,000 students.

Vannes, beside the Gulf of Morbihan, retains behind its ramparts picturesque old quarters, and its small port is a point of departure for boat trips. At the mouth of the Odet Estuary, **Quimper**, the ancient capital of Cornwall, is the city which remains the most Breton of the region. Its narrow lanes running from old houses lead to the Cathedral of Saint-Corentin.

Saint-Brieuc, close to the sea, is primarily an administrative and commercial centre, the exhibitions and markets of which have an influence on the entire department.

The Pink Granite Coast *is like a stack of oddly shaped rocks. by following the "chemin des douaniers", the stroller attempts to find, in all this chaos of granite, the "rabbit", the "tortoise", and the "mushroom"... (Côtes-d'Armor.)*

Saint-Malo *as from the 16th century, ensured its prosperity by taking part in the Canadian fur trade, and fishing for cod in the waters off Newfoundland. Ferries connect it with the south of England. (Ille-et-Vilaine.)*

The head-dress *makes for the originality of the traditional Breton costume. The Bigouden head-dress is that of a high cylindrical lace, and is without doubt the most original. (Finistère.)*

The granite rocks of Huelgoat *are one of the strangest sites in inland Brittany. They form, along with the neighbouring forest, a much visited excursion centre with evocative names: the Devil's Grotto, the Chaos of the Mill... (Finistère.)*

The jube of the Saint-Fiacre-du-Faouët Chapel *is a masterpiece of high polychrome wood art. (Morbihan.)*

The Brasparts Calvary, *in the heart of the Arrée Mountains possesses one of the most moving pieta in Brittany. (Finistère.)*

Centre

The Central region of France, also known as the Centre-Val de Loire, is located at the heart of France, a bridge between regions as distant from each other as Normandy and the Auvergne, the Limousin and the Greater Paris Area. To the north the Eure-et-Loire countryside is dominated by extended areas of cereal cultivation which have something in common with the Paris Basin. **Chartres**, as a result of the spires of its cathedral, is visible from a long distance across this immense sea of wheat. The cathedral's sculptured decor consists of 4,000 figures, and its collection of stained-glass windows depicts 5,000 individuals.

The château at Villandry *is famous for its gardens, including the varied coloured seasonal vegetable patch, the result of medieval monastic gardens. It is completely renewed twice per annum. (Indre-et-Loire.)*

Chambord, *built by François 1st from 1519 onwards is the largest of the Loire chateaux. Of perfect architectural consistency it has 440 rooms accessed by 83 staircases. (Loir-et-Cher.)*

The Indre-et-Loire, the Loir-et-Cher and the Loiret are washed by the Loire, the longest river in France. On its course **Tours** (the cathedral of Saint-Gatien), the major Loire valley city. **Blois**, the château of which is located in the city centre and was designed by Louis XIIth, François 1st and Gaston d'Orléans, and **Orléans** (Sainte-Croix cathedral), the capital of medieval France.

Since the north wing was demolished in during the 18th century, the courtyard of the **Château de Chaumont** *overlooks the Loire River. It was one this spot that Henry II Plantagenêt had his last meeting with Thomas Becket before this last was murdered at Canterbury. (Loir-et-Cher.)*

The Indre and the Cher Departments, to the south make up the Berry, one of the oldest agricultural regions of France. This is a slightly raised, extensive, and highly fertile plateau, to the south of which is hill country. To the east, the Sancerrois area is famous for its vines which flourish on banks of chalk.

The old quarters of **Bourges**, and its cathedral, at the heart of the Champagne Berry area remind one of its rich medieval past. During the 12th century the city was an archbishopric, an advanced post of the Kingdom faced with the territories of the South West dominated by the inhabitants of Anjou. **Châteauroux**, a communications crossroads, is an active industrial city (mechanics, farm produce) which retains a medieval part of town.

The modest hamlet of Nohant *has an elegant 18th century residence, made famous by its owner George Sand (1804-1876), who had as guests Chopin, Delacroix, Liszt... (Indre.)*

The Notre-Dame-de-la-Belle-Verrière *is one of the most precious of the stained glass windows in Chartres Cathedral: the radiant blue of the central panels (12th century) enhances the more intense blues used by the 13th century master. (Eure-et-Loire.)*

Bourges, Saint-Etienne Cathedral *(1200-1270): the visitor can, if located at the end of the building, between the last two pillars, be profoundly affected by the formidable vertical impulse of the choir, the vaults of which are 37 meters from the ground. (Cher.)*

The Saint-Gatien Cathedral at Tours *has a remarkable flamboyant facade: festoon archivolts, ornamental leaf gables. (Indre-et-Loire.)*

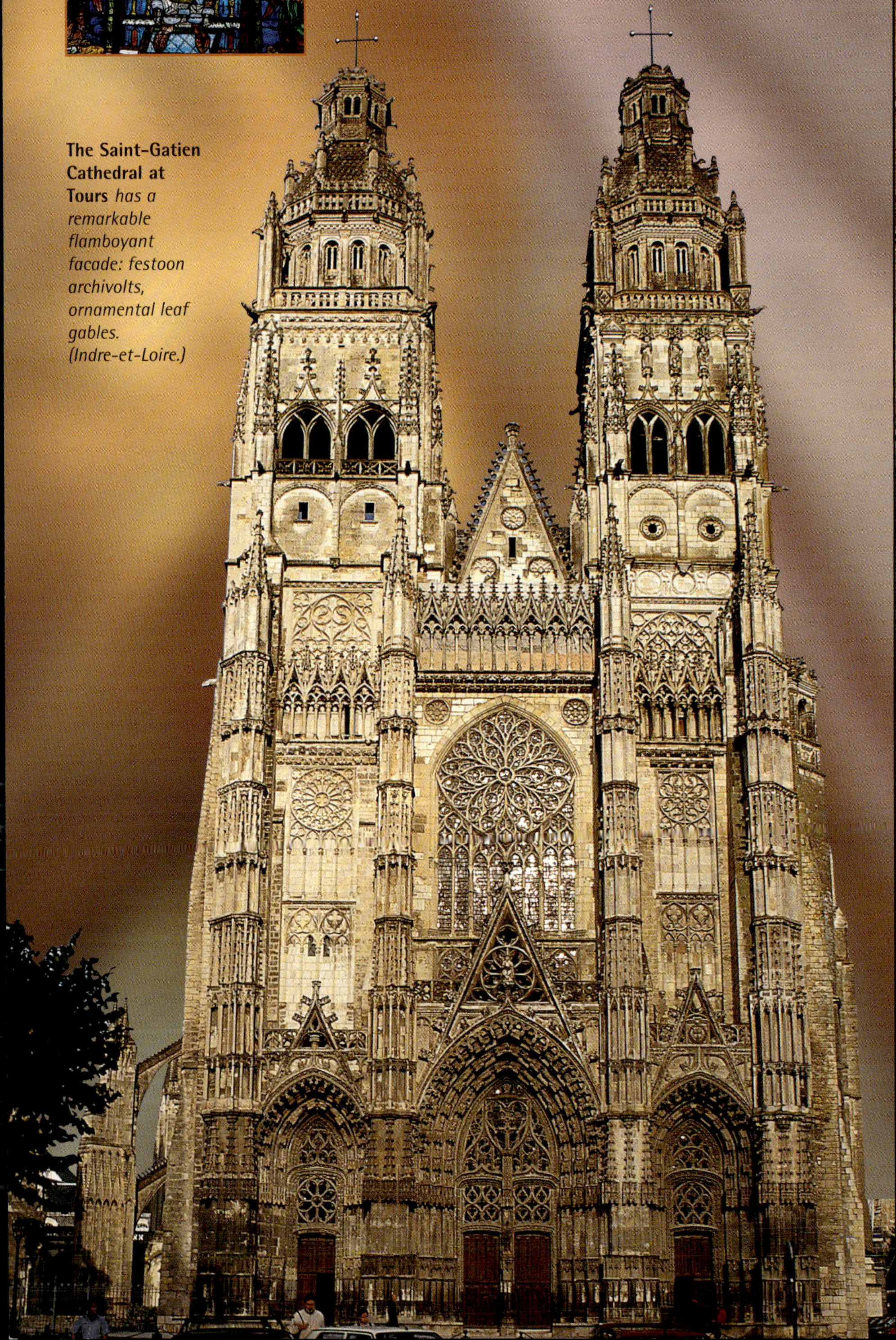

The Noirlac Benedictine Abbey, *in the Cher Valley, remains the most complete and best preserved monastic setting in France. The, end of 13th century, multifoiled, gothic cloister has fine small columns, the capitals of which are decorated with plants. (Cher.)*

Founded in 650, **the abbey of Saint-Benoît-sur-Loire** *was destroyed during the French Revolution. All that remains is the remarkable abbey church preceded by a huge 9th century tower porch of Carthaginian influence. (Loiret.)*

Champagne-Ardenne

At the heart of the Champagne area, on the slopes of the Marne valley and to the south of Epernay, flourishes the famous Champagne wine growing area which exports its production throughout the entire world. **Reims**, the city of coronations, owes its fame to two major monuments: the Roman basilica of Saint-Remi, and the Gothic cathedral, the facade of which is one of the most beautiful in France. The city contains numerous Champagne cellars, which are open to the public. From **Châlons-en-Champagne** to **Troyes** stretches a huge plain (chalky Champagne), devoted to the large scale agricultural production of cereals and beets. Châlons, crossed by the the Mau and Nau canals which originate in the Marne river, has very pretty 17th and 18th century hotels, and timber frame houses. The ancient capital of Champagne, Troyes has preserved a beautiful old quarter with numerous churches, along with a cathedral of impressive dimensions.

Towards the east and south the countryside becomes more irregular around Bar-sur-Aube and Bar-sur-Seine, then the immense Langres' plateau appears. Being at the junction of several roads, **Chaumont** has played an active commercial role since the Middle Ages.

The small wine producing market town of Hautvilliers, *in the heart of the Champagne wine area, has elegant wrought iron signs. (Marne.)*

The Castellane Champagne cellars *at Epernay, extend over 10 kilometres. A museum devoted to the Champagne Tradition enables the work of cellarmen and coopers to be discovered. (Marne.)*

Troyes Cathedral *is a major work of Champagne gothic, undertaken in 1208. The nave is a remarkable three floor erection, of total openwork design. (Aube.)*

The Ardennes, to the north, are a primary massif covered with forests and crossed by the meandering Meuse river. Charleville-Mézières, the administrative and commercial city, has not forgotten the poet Arthur Rimbaud.

The Notre-Dame-en-Vaux cloister's museum, *at Châlons-en-Champagne, exhibits 12th century sculptures which decorated a cloister which was discovered in 1960. (Marne.)*

The statue of the Ange au sourire *(Smiling Angel) on the facade of* **Reims** *Cathedral, reveals a Champagne style of architecture characterised by visual vivacity, and liberty of attitude. (Marne.)*

Corsica

Corsica is the highest of the Mediterranean islands, reaching 2,706 meters at its highest point at the Monte Cinto. Its 1,000 km of rocky coast are deeply indented, alternating between deep gulfs, small creeks, and tapering headlands. In the interior, the mountains and high valleys are sprinkled with picturesque perched villages.

Bastia, to the north of the island, was, throughout the occupation by Genoa during the war of independence (1729-1769) towards the end of the 14th century, the administrative and financial capital of Corsica. The city developed on each side of the old port, the large houses which are at the bottom of the mountain composing an attractive scene.

The archeological site at Filitosa has pre-historic remains which contain a wealth of information regarding this period of history: the menhir statues were carved about 1500 B.C. by the Toréens, a sea going people who settled the land.

Ajaccio is an ancient Genoese colony situated in the hollow of a superb gulf. The city experienced considerable development during the 18th century, and is the place where Napoléon Bonaparte was born in 1769.

The church of San Michele at Murato *(1280) is a fine example of pisan Roman art. It is recognisable by its polychromic bonding of alternating white limestone moellons, and dark green serpentine. (Haute-Corse.)*

The **Filitosa** *menhirs statues. (Corse-du-Sud.)*

The Gulf of Porto and the Scandola natural reserve *with their pink granite cliffs plunging vertically into the blue sea are the most spectacular natural sites in Corsica. (Corse-du-Sud.)*

Saint-Florent and its marina *are superbly located in the hollow of a very beautiful gulf. (Corse-du-Sud.)*

Franche-Comté

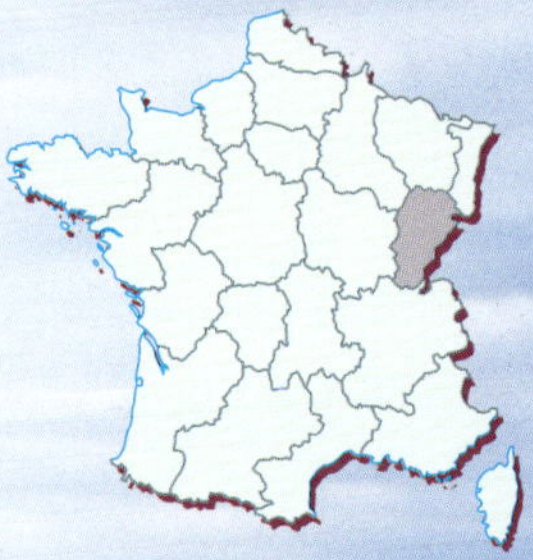

The Franche-Comté consists of three distinct entities. To the east, the mountains and the high plateaux of the Jura form a crescent oriented from the south towards the north east, an alternation of dark fir tree forests, and extensive pastures. Water is to be seen everywhere, in the form of torrents, water falls, springs, and resurgences. The freshness and beauty of the scenery has been praised by numerous poets, i.e. Ruskin, the Englishman, Goethe the German, and Lamartine, French. To the west, a huge plateau, crossed by the Saône river, is demarcated to the north by the rounded tops of the Vosges covered with superb forests.

The Franche-Comté is reputed for its production of dairy products, pride of place going to the comté, a gruyère type cheese which has matured in cellars known as fruitières for between six to eight months.

Besançon has an original location in the middle of a loop in the Doubs river, overlooked by steep hills the strategic importance of which did not go unnoticed by Cesar. Vauban, on the order of Louis XIV, had a formidable stronghold built, which can still be visited today. Besançon is the French capital of the clock and watch making industry.

The **Belfort** Gap, accessed by the railway, motorway, and the Rhône-Rhine canal, links the Rhenish country and, beyond that of the Franche-Comté, and the south of France. Since time immemorial this has been the route of the invader.

The High Plateaux of the Jura *is an ideal spot to practice cross country skiing. The Great Jura Crossing – Grande Traversée du Jura (GTJ)—is marked out over 250 kilometres. (Doubs, Jura.)*

The old royal salt works at Arc-et-Senans *is one of the last example of end of 18th century industrial architecture. This "ideal" city was designed by Claude-Nicolas Ledoux. (Doubs.)*

The Château at Joux *dominates the Pontarlier valley, an access used since time immemorial. It was built during the 11 century by the Joux nobility who levied a toll for right of way. (Doubs.)*

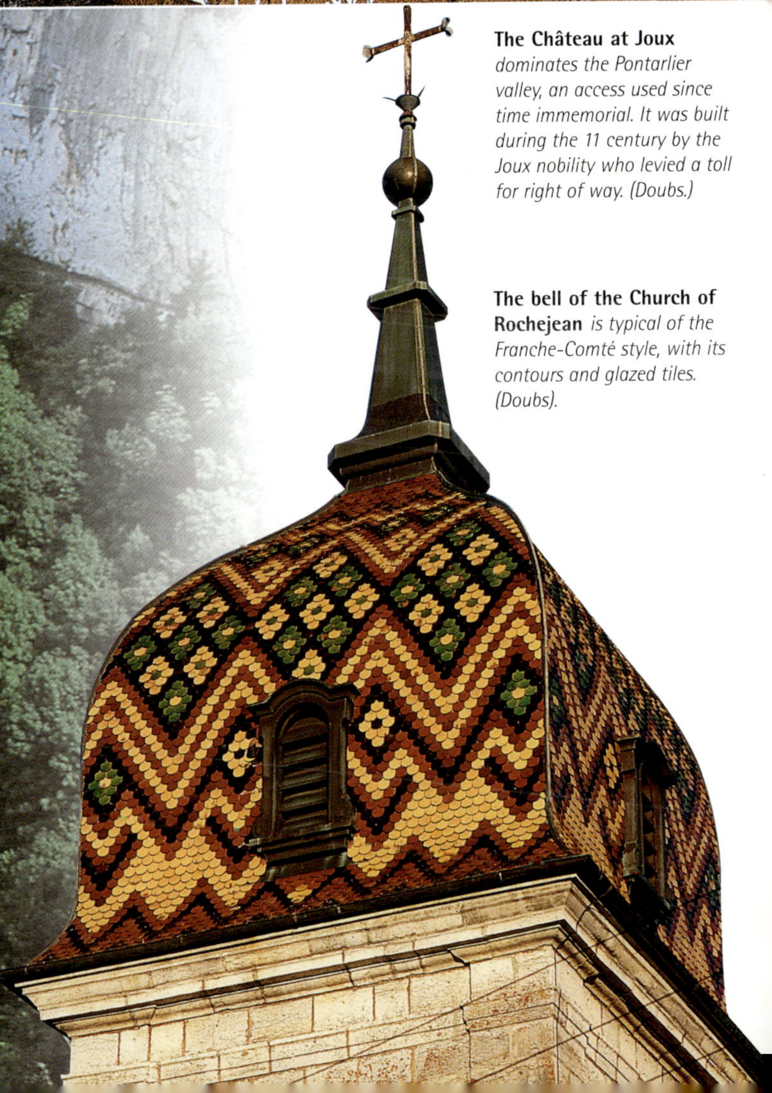

The bell of the Church of Rochejean *is typical of the Franche-Comté style, with its contours and glazed tiles. (Doubs).*

The Greater Paris Area

Ever since the Capetians made it their capital in the 12th century, Paris has seen the erection of numerous prestigious monuments, which give witness to its economic and political importance. The cathedral of Notre Dame on the Ile de la Cité, with its wonderful proportional equilibrium is one of the finest examples of French gothic in existence. The Champs-Elysées, lined by the head offices of major companies, and luxury shopping, runs from the Place de la Concorde to the Arc de Triomphe which was raised on the orders of Napoléon. The Eiffel Tower, built to commemorate the Universal Exhibition of 1889, is one of the masterpieces of metal construction, a combination of lightness of form ,and strength. Montmartre, dominated by the church of the Sacré-Cœur, during the last century, and until 1914, was the favourite part of town for authors and artists. Political power resides in the Elysée Palace (the President of the Republic), at the Palais-Bourbon (the National Assembly), and the Luxembourg Palais (the Senat).

The Pont Neuf, *the oldest bridge in Paris, was the first to have sidewalks. It consists of two bridges separated by a statue of Henry IV. (París.)*

The Cathedral of Notre-Dame *was built between 1163 and 1345, the wonderful equilibrium of its proportions makes it one of the most beautiful of French gothic examples. (Paris.)*

With its railway stations and airports, Paris is an international communications crossroads where the High Speed Rail Network, and numerous motorways converge.
The châteaux, parks, and cathedrals of the Greater Paris Area are also evocative of a rich historical past. The château at Versailles being representative of the absolute power of royalty during the reign of Louis XIV. The château at Fontainebleau has been converted, and lived in, by every French sovereign from the 13th century to Napoléon III, whilst the basilica of Saint-Denis contains the tombs of almost all the Kings of France, from Dagobert to Louis XVIII.
A surround of forests and magnificent valleys (Seine, Oise, Marne) give this region, which has seen the development of numerous new towns, a certain appeal.

Crowning the hill of Montmartre, the **Sacré-Cœur** *was built after the defeat of 1870. It is a pastiche of Byzantine art. (Paris.)*

The Place de la Concorde *has for centrepiece one of the Luxor obelisks which was offered to France by the viceroy of Egypt Mehemet-Ali during the visit of Jean-François Champollion, in 1829. The Place was arranged by Gabriel from 1755 to 1775. Two hotels with beautiful colonnades line the rue Royale. (Paris.)*

From the top of the Eiffel Tower Paris and its monuments are overlooked:
here, the Grand Palais, the Place de la Concorde, the church of La Madeleine, and the Opera. In the foreground the bridges of les Invalides and that of Alexander III. (Paris.)

The Mirror Room at the Château at Versailles *is one huge 75 meter long reception room. Seventeen large windows give out onto the park with their seventeen panels comprising 578 mirrors. This gallery was used for major court ceremonies and celebrations. Proclamation of the German Empire was made their on January 18th 1871, and the treaty of Versailles signed on June 28, 1919. (Yvelines.)*

The château of Vaux-le-Vicomte *is one of the most beautiful successes of 17th century classical architecture. It was raised by Louis Le Vau for Nicolas Fouquet, Lord High Treasurer to Louis XIV. The monument is an integral part of a huge landscaped assembly designed by Le Nôtre, including paths, ornamental ponds, and statues. (Seine-et-Marne.)*

The Louvre, a onetime palace of French kings, *it was made into a museum during the 18th century with the opening to the public of the "Grande Galerie". The main entrance is via the pyramid in glass designed by I. M. Pei. The six departments of the museum deal with all major artistic periods from Antiquity to the 19th century (Paris.)*

The first large department stores *were built at the end of the 19th century: Printemps and the Galeries Lafayette having huge halls lit by glass roofs supported by metal frames. (Paris.)*

The area of **La Défense** at the gates of Paris, is a business area comprising tower blocks arranged around a vast open space. Escalators lead to the "Grande Arche" where there is a fine outlook onto the La Défense development, with on the left the CNIT which consists of 80,000 square meters of covered surface area. (Hauts-de-Seine.)

The Georges Pompidou Centre *(National Centre for Art and Culture) was designed by the architects Rogers and Piano who used steel framework, and partitions in glass. Here can be found a public information library, the Centre for Industrial Creation, the Institute for Research and Acoustics' Co-ordination (IRCAM), and the National Museum of Modern Art. (Paris.)*

Languedoc-Roussillon

The vast Languedoc-Roussillon region is a collection of a great variety of landscapes, from the high plateaux of the Aubrac Lozère, to the rugged banks of the Côte Vermeille. To the north the Gorges du Tarn deeply gouges the extensive sheep grazed limestone plateaux. Grottoes and chasms are evidence of the slow wear of running water. The Cévennes range of mountains appear like a series of heavy granite summits covered with a dark mantle of forest. More to the south the scenery becomes Mediterranean, and the vine is increasingly to be seen

The Benedictine abbey of Saint-Martin-du-Canigou *is located at a site the altitude of which is 1,094 meters. The buildings, which were constructed during the 11th century, have three cloister galleries remaining (the fourth, which opens out onto the mountain, has been restored), and the church with its massive keep like steeple. (Pyrénées-Orientales.)*

on the mellow slopes of the Hérault and the Aude Valley. Lastly, the Corbières area, an immense patchwork of orchards and vineyards, and the Fenouillèdes give way to the Roussillon overlooked by the heights of the Pyrenees.

Located in the narrow threshold which separates the Massif Central from the Pyrenees, the prosperity of the fortified city of **Carcassonne** is based on the wine trade. **Perpignan**, the principle city of the Roussillon, with its warm and vivacious atmosphere is evocative of nearby Catalonia. **Montpellier**, for a long time, had profited from the trade in spices with the Eastern Mediterranean prior to becoming, during the reign of Louis XIV, the administrative capital of Lower Languedoc. The old quarter of Montpellier has fine monuments dating from the 17th and 18th centuries. Between Garrigue and the Costière du Gard, **Nîmes** continues to be marked by Gallo-Roman antiquity: one should see the arenas, the Maison Carrée and, a few kilometres to the north east, the Pont du Gard which carries across the Gardon valley an aqueduct which supplies Nîmes with fresh spring water. In the middle of a huge expanse of marshland and lakes, **Aigues-Mortes** was founded by Saint-Louis anxious to possess a stronghold on the Mediterranean coastline.

The Fenouillèdes *is hard countryside of average size mountains located between the region of Corbières and Roussillon. Its slopes, covered with scrubland and holm oak, give way at times to the vine. (Pyrénées-Orientales.)*

The Palace of the Kings of Majorca *is a reminder of the time when Perpignan, during the 14th and 15th centuries, was the advanced post of Catalan civilisation north of the Pyrenees. Today, it is a commercial, highly vivacious, city the dynamism of which lies partially in the export of fruit and wines produced close by. (Pyrénées-Orientales.)*

Peyrepertuse, *perched on a rocky spur, is the largest of the cathar châteaux. A refuge for the Cathars, it fell after three days of combat in November 1240. Saint Louis made it the main stronghold facing the region of Roussillon. (Aude.)*

The old village of **Saint-Guilhem-le-Désert** *is gathered around the old abbey, at the outlet of wild gorges. The 9th century abbey church has a highly ornate chevet. The apse is crowned by arcades separated by fine small columns. (Hérault.)*

Located in a tight sill which separates the Massif Central from the Pyrenees, **the city of Carcassonne** controls the route from the Atlantic to the Mediterranean, and between France and Spain. At around 1130, Trencavel nobility built their fortified château.(p. 6). The fortress was annexed by France as a result of the Albigensian Crusade (1224-1226). Louis IX then Philippe le Hardi constructed a second external boundary which made the place practically attack proof. (Aude.)

Fontfroide Abbey nestles at the hollow of a small Corbières' valley populated with cypress trees and arbutus. In 1093, several monks in search for a place to pray founded this monastery, which, in 1143, became part of the order of Cistercians. In the Middle Ages Fontfroide was to be a bulwark of orthodoxy confronted by Catharism. (Aude.)

It was **the Pont du Gard** *which conveyed, across the valley of the River Gardon, 20,000 cubic meters of water, via a 49 kilometre long aqueduct from a spring close to Uzès to Nîmes. Constructed in 19 B.C. by the Romans, it superposes three levels of arcade composed of enormous moellons. (Gard.)*

Rising above the middle of a vast area of marshes and lakes, **Aigues-Mortes** *was created by Saint Louis, for the purposes of having a stronghold on the Mediterranean coastline along with a place for departure for the crusades. (Gard.)*

The Gorges du Tarn *are a deep gash in the extensive limestone plateaux which cover the south east of the Massif Central. The river has used a series of natural rifts to clear a way through. (Lozère.)*

The Fenestrelle Tower *gives witness to the medieval past of Uzès. (Gard.)*

Limousin

Surrounding Limoges the landscape is one of average hills consisting of hedges and grazing land, the home of the Limousin cattle, divided up by copses of oak, beech, and chestnut trees. **Limoges**, the administrative and university city, owes its fame to the manufacture of its porcelain of renown.

To the south east lies the Millavaches plateau a scattering of stony areas exposed to the wind and plentiful rainfall which acts as a source of water for numerous rivers (Creuse, Vienne, Corrèze...). This rough environment explains its very low population. Around **Guéret**, and the Marche, a countryside made up of wooded valleys and grazing, is one of transition from the Val de Loire and The Massif Central. Capital of the Comté de la Marche during the 13th century, Guéret has retained its position as administrative centre, whilst Aubusson owes its prosperity to the clear waters of the River Creuse which encouraged the development of the tanning industry, and later of tapestry-making.

Between the Vézère and Dordogne are the plateaux of the Lower Limousin, the granite soil of which has been gouged by the Corrèze river and above all the Dordogne river descending from the Massif Central. **Brive-la-Gaillarde** is an

Brive-la-Gaillarde *owes its name to the number of sieges it suffered. The Hôtel de Labenche is the most beautiful building in the city. It's style is that of typical Toulouse Renaissance. (Corrèze.)*

Limoges is universally known for its china.
The Adrien-Dubouché museumexhibits more than 10,000 pieces originating from manufacturers throughout the entire world. (Haute-Vienne.)

Quite close to the Millevaches plateau, **Meymac** *has retained intact its old houses which are gathered around the 12th-13th century abbey church. Its chevet is of restrained appearance (Corrèze.)*

active town (canning, food produce), located in the middle of an enormous basin given over to the cultivation of fruit and market garden produce. **Tulle** is situated in an original location on the steep slopes of the Corrèze River, overlooked by the cathedral of Notre-Dame, the remains of a one time abbey.

The Millevaches Plateau (thousand springs) *is the water tower of the Limousin. Its granite heights are moors covered with heather, ferns, and broken up by a few forests. (Corrèze, Creuse.)*

The Merle Towers *(13th century) did not resist the arrival of artillery, which, from the heights, could bombard them without difficulty. (Corrèze.)*

The old houses of Turenne *are tightly grouped around the château. The Viscount of Turenne, during the 15th century, had more than 1,200 villages under his control. (Corrèze.)*

The church of the old Abbaye of Moutier-d'Ahun *contains a surprising collection of sculptured panelling and stalls dating from between 1673 and 1683 by Simon Baüer, the artist from Auvergne. (Creuse.)*

Lorraine

The region of the Lorraine consists of plateaux, slightly inclining towards the west, and the eastern slopes of the Jura mountains. To the north these plateaux are broken up by a succession of north south running hilly inclines covered with forests and bottom ground consisting of both grazing and arable land. A frontier region, Lorraine has for a long time been influenced by the hostility of European Nations, as the remains of past battles and fortifications give witness. Struck by the decline in traditional industry (mining, and steel), Lorraine has undergone considerable readjustment characterised by a concern for diversification. **Nancy**, the ancient capital of the Duchy of Lorraine, has retained its remarkable architectural heritage surrounding the Place Stanislas, a perfect example of elegance and equilibrium. **Metz**, for a long time was a religious metropolis, and a first category military establishment. The city is dominated by the Cathedral of Saint-Etienne.

To the south, the mountains of the Vosges are covered with a thick cover of forest which thins out, then disappears above 1,000 meters to become stubble land which is covered with snow during the winter. The plain which extends to the west of the Vosges is especially endowed with hot springs: **Vittel** and **Contrexéville** being two of the most well known spars.

Metz, *the ancient capital of Lotharingie, has always been a religious city and place of utmost military importance being close to the Franco-German border. (Moselle.)*

The Lunéville pottery works, *one time royal manufacturer, produced for the most part china for the table. The finest examples can be admired at the museum located in the château. Here, the "Baby", King Stanislas dwarf. (Meuthe-et-Moselle.)*

Ancient capital of the Dukes of Lorraine, **Nancy** *has retained a remarkable architectural heritage. The Place Stanislas is a perfect example of elegance and equilibrium which was characteristic of the French 18th century. Stanislas Leszczynski, father in law of Louis XV, decided in 1752 to develop an area which was intended to reunite the old quarter of Nancy with the new town. The close co-operation between Emmanuel Héré, the architect, and Jean Lamour, the genius wrought iron craftsman grants the whole a rare harmony. (Meurthe-et-Moselle.)*

The Lorraine slopes of the Vosges mountains *are covered with a thick covering of forest, and are part of the Vosges Ballons Regional Park. (Vosges.)*

Midi-Pyrénées

The Midi-Pyrénées join together on both sides of the Garonne river passage, very distinct geographical entities, from the Pyrenees to the south and to the foothills of the Massif Central to the north.

The Pyrenean mountain chain raises its snowy peaks and ragged crests above hanging valleys covered with forests and extended pastures. This is the playground of the rambler and winter sports, and spectacular sites like the amphitheatre at Gavarnie.

Valleys running from north to south demarcate countryside of well defined character: the Bigorre and the Comminges areas are rolling countryside which is dotted with white houses, the Ariège with its cave riddled slopes. **Tarbes**, **Saint-Gaudens** and **Foix** are small flourishing towns where life is good, and form a link between the hard mountain climate, and the milder Gascon countryside. At its centre lie the hills of Armagnac the home of the famous eau-de-vie the distilling process of which requires the greatest of care.

The Garonne countryside, on each side of the river, rises in terraces covered with huge orchards, vines, and cereals. **Toulouse**, with its superb monuments (the Basilica of Saint-Sernin, the Jacobins' cloister) is built in brick, hence its name

The Pyrenees Mountain Chain *extends, over approximately 500 kilometres, from the Atlantic to the Mediterranean. The central portion bristles with granite outcrops such as the Néouvielle massif, formed by glacial erosion. (Hautes-Pyrénées)*

At the heart of the Ariège Department, *the Ancient Château of the Counts of Foix has retained its defensive watch towers. (Ariège.)*

of the "pink city", and is a highly active regional city, famous for aeronautic and aerospace construction.

Further to the north the vines of Albi (**Gaillac** wine) are planted around villages crowned with little knolls. The Grands Causses, vast stony arid limestone plateaux, the home of sheep, cover part of the Aveyron. Finally, Rouergue and Upper Quercy alternate their wooded and limestone plateaux with steep-sided valleys. Numerous caves attract potholing enthusiasts, whilst for those interested in the dawn of humanity (prehistoric engravings, and rock art).

The Midi Peak at Bigorre *stands out above the Pyrenees at 2,865 meters. On the summit is an observatory and scientific research institute. (Hautes-Pyrénées.)*

The Cathedral of Sainte-Marie at Auch, *stalls carved between 1500 and 1552. (Gers.)*

Toulouse *owes to brick, the most used material in the construction of its monuments, its other name of the "pink city". The "Place du Capitole" is the favourite meeting place for the people of Toulouse. (Haute-Garonne.)*

During the 13th century **Albi** *sheltered followers of the Cathar sect who were persecuted by the forces of the Inquisition. Its cathedral, Saint Cécile, started in 1282, has the appearance of a fortress. (Tarn.)*

The Abbey at Moissac, *founded during the 7th century, reached its most influential period during the 11th and 12th centuries. It is from this period that the cloister with fine marble columns supporting very varied chapiters dates. (Tarn-et-Garonne.)*

The treasure of the Sainte-Foy-de-Conques church *exhibits the striking 10th century statue and relic of Saint Foy, recovered with gold and precious stones. (Aveyron.)*

Lautrec, *an ancient fortified place with a picturesque maze of little streets lined with old houses, it is famous for its incomparably flavoured pink garlic.* (Tarn.)

The old houses of Estaing, *on the banks of the River Lot, are overlooked by the château which was built between the 15th and 16th centuries. (Lot*

Rocamadour, *with its dwellings, sanctuaries, tourelles and fortified gates sticking to the cliff face, is one of the most visited sites in France. (Lot.)*

The Lot has dug its bed over the Quercy plateaux *and runs between the steep slopes of hard limestone covered with chestnut groves. (Lot.)*

Nord-Pas-de-Calais

The central part of the Pas-de-Calais consists of the Artois hills which separate the flat lands of Lens and Arras from the Boulonnais, a countryside of thickets and whitewashed farms. **Boulogne** remains the first ranking fishing port of France. To the north, is the Côte d'Opale area, cape Blanc-Nez and cape Gris-Nez, which are at the extremity of the limestone plateau from which the tunnel under the English Channel was excavated. **Calais**, located only 38 km from England, is the first ranking port of France for passenger traffic.

The Grand-Place at Arras *is a unique collection of Flemish style 17th and 18th century houses supported by arcades intended to protect market traders and customers from inclement weather. (Pas-de-Calais.)*

Lille takes advantage of its geographical position *to become, at the centre of the North-South axis, one of the large European metropolises. The "Place Général De Gaulle" (Main Square) is the centre of Lille life. (Nord.)*

Boulogne *is the first ranking port in continental Europe for fresh fish, and boats come to berth alongside the Gambetta wharf. (Pas-de-Calais.)*

The Côte d'Opale *between Cape Blanc-Nez and Cape Gris-Nez. (Pas-de-Calais.)*

A major portion of the North consists of the Flanders' plain which for a long time lived with the high furnaces, and slag heaps of the black country cohabiting with sprawling agricultural land. Brick construction is to be seen everywhere, from the modest dwellings of workers, to public buildings, and churches, the belfries of which dot the countryside.

Lille has taken advantage of its geographical position to become one of the major European urban areas, served by ultra efficient communi-cations i.e. the High Speed Train (TGV). However, its rich past is not forgotten, and the enhancement of its historic centre makes visible those periods when it was, in turn, Flemish, Austrian, Spanish, and finally under Louis XIV, French.

To the east at Hainaut and Cambrésis wheat and beetroot are cultivated on plains of chalk broken up by hedged valleys.

Being 38 kilometres from the coast of England, **Calais** *channels the major portion of traffic to the British Isles which use the tunnel under the Channel, or the numerous ferries. Its belfry rises to 75 metres. (Pas-de-Calais.)*

Lower Normandy

Part of Lower Normandy is the plain of Caen which is given over to wide scale cultivation and bordered to the north by a straight coast line, and the Cotentin peninsular, the northern part of the Armoricain Massif, consisting of rolling pasture land squared in by hedgerows. The west coast is of varied appearance: cliffs of granite, dunes, and beaches of sand, and the bay of the Mont-Saint-Michel. Further to the south the parkland of Normandie-Maine and the Perche are charming with their wooded hills, and small valleys.

The charming little 16th century château of **Saint-Germain-de-Livet**, *nestling amongst the thickets of Normandy is like a checkerboard of coloured stone and brick. (Calvados.)*

Caen is both an industrial centre and a port which is linked to the sea by the Orne minor canal. The Abbaye aux Hommes founded by William the Conqueror in 1066, and the Abbaye aux Dames founded by his wife Mathilde, are the city's architectural jewels. At Bayeux, it is essential to see the 50 meter long tapestry created in the 11th century and which depicts the dispute of William and Harold for the crown of England.

Honfleur, *with its old dock lined with straight and high slate dressed houses has inspired numerous painters and poets: Boudin, Corot, Baudelaire...(Calvados.)*

From **Honfleur**, with its harbour surrounded by high straight tile covered houses, to Barfleur, a charming fishing port at the very end of the Cotentin peninsular, are scattered resorts, and the long beaches selected for the landing on June 6, 1944 by the allied armies. The Pays d'Auge, a region of valleys and hedges is famous for its cheeses (Camembert, Livarot, Pont-l'évêque) and its cider.

An original site, a thousand year old history, and an architecture as beautiful as it is audacious has resulted in the **Mont-Saint-Michel** *being named a "Wonder of the West". (Manche.)*

To the north west of the Contentin peninsula, the **Nez de Jobourg** *is a steep headland surrounded by reefs. (Manche.)*

Upper Normandy

Upper Normandy is shared by the Seine Valley: to the north of the river lies the Pays de Caux, a chalk plateau surrounded by high cliffs, whilst the Pays de Bray is a nest of verdant pasture specialised in dairy production.

To the south the Pays d'Ouche, with its forests and pasture land, opens out onto the huge treeless plains of Neubourg and **Evreux** which are entirely given over to the growing of cereals.

Rouen, an important maritime and river port, retains from its past numerous monuments of considerable interest (the cathedral, the law courts). The "Golden Age" of the Norman Capital (middle of the 14th century – beginning of the 16th century) was a prosperous period of, in the main, merchants dealing with ship owners for trade on the new maritime routes. The port of Le Havre is a major place of trade, at the mouth of the valley of the River Seine where numerous industries are located.

The central square at **Ferrière-sur-Risle** *has picturesque old timber frame houses. (Eure.)*

The château at Les Andelys (Château-Gaillard) *occupies a strategic position overlooking the River Seine, and access to Rouen. (Seine-Maritime.)*

Etretat, an elegant seaside resort, is surrounded by spectacular chalk cliffs. **Fécamp** is devoted to fishing and trade, whilst **Dieppe** is both the oldest of seaside resorts in France, and has the closest beach to Paris.

The cliffs at Côte d'Albâtre and Le Tréport, *on the River Bresle estuary which marks the northern limit of Normandy. (Seine-Maritime.)*

The law courts at Rouen *were built during the "Golden Century" of the capital of Normandy (second half of the 15th century), in the Renaissance period style. (Seine-Maritime.)*

The arch known as the "Porte d'Aval et l'Aiguille" *made famous by Arsène Lupin, hero of the novel by Maurice Leblanc,* **L'Aiguille Creuse**, *are an integral part of the spectacular Cliffs at Etretat. (Seine Maritime.)*

The Loire Valley

In the north of the area the Lower Maine has a marked aspect of hedged pasture land. It could be called the Black Maine because of its houses constructed out of granite and shale, whilst the White Maine derives from the limestone soil basin of the River Huisne and River Sarthe. The old quarter of **Laval** is located on a hillside overlooking the Mayenne. **Le Mans** is a busy city (manufacturing and insurance), known world wide for its annual automobile race (the 24 Hour Race at Le Mans).

The Anjou area, which extends from both side of the Loire, between **Saumur** and Saint-Florent, is known for the mildness of its climate and the harmony of its landscape which shelters many châteaux and abbeys (Montgeoffroy, Fontevraud, Serrant, Brissac...) Washed by the waters of the River Maine, **Angers** is known for its architecture which ranges from white tufa to slate. The city deals in the famous Anjou wines, and has developed a considerable high technology industry.

The historic centre of Le Mans *has been completely restored. The "Deux-Amis" house is a typical example of Middle Age architecture. (Sarthe.)*

The Brière Regional National Park, *to the north of the River Loire estuary, protects a vast marsh drained and dried by the persistent work of man. The marsh is totally accessible as a result of a network of canals. (Loire-Atlantique.)*

Epau Abbey, *close to Le Mans,* *was founded in 1229 by Queen Bérangère, widow of Richard the Lion Heart. The chapter room has elegant diagonal rib arches. (Sarthe.)*

Nantes, the ancient city of the Dukes of Brittany, is today the region's capital. Located at the spot where the River Loire enters the sea it had been able to trade with both Lower Brittany, the Poitou area, and more distant places. Its château, protected externally by strong towers surrounded by moats, has on the side facing the court yard an elegant Renaissance facade.

To the north of the estuary, the Grande Brière area is a vast marsh drained and dried by the persistent work of men. The Vendée has the twin attractions of both its immense beaches of white sand, and the charm of its inland country where hedged land predominates, and where the hills are sometimes crowned with wind mills. The Isle of **Noirmoutier** has the attraction of its beaches along with the offer of quiet woods, and salt marshes.

The château of Angers, *with the massive towers of its surrounding wall, is an interesting example of feudal architecture. It houses a wall covering depicting the Apocalypse, the oldest and largest (135 meters), which can only be admired. (Maine-et-Loire.)*

Saint-Gilles-Croix-de-Vie *is a community which is firmly oriented towards the sea, and where the activities of tourism and fishing exist together harmoniously. (Vendée.)*

The extent of the marshes, along with strong sunlight enables salt marsh workers to harvest salt from about a hundred kilometres of the **Noirmoutier marshes.** *(Vendée.)*

The large beach at **Sables-d'Olonne***, splendid coastal resort on the Vendée coast.*

Its mild climate, the pure Atlantic air, a preserved natural environment, along with numerous beaches make **Noirmoutier** *highly sought after by holiday makers. (Vendée.)*

Picardy

The immense extent of the Picardy plateau, interspersed with valleys and lakes, are covered with fields of cereals and beets. **Amiens** is renowned for its cathedral the dimensions of which are exceptional and result in it being the largest gothic edifice in France.

Between **Abbeville** and the sea, the bay of the **Somme** river at low tide reveals huge wild spaces covered with grass and sand, a favourite observation area for nature lovers.

To the east the department of Aisne contains the region of Thiérache with its interesting fortified churches, and the vast open spaces dominated by the cathedrals of **Laon** and **Soissons**.

Between **Compiègne** and **Senlis**, the Valois offers its forests as one of the lungs of the neighbouring Greater Paris Area. For those interested in examples of French history and architecture visits to **Pierrefonds, Compiègne, Chaalis, and Chantilly** are essential. **Beauvais**, the ancient Gallo-Roman capital, is dominated by the cathedral of Saint-Pierre, unfinished as a result of successive collapse. The choir, the vaults of which rise to almost 50 meters, has an incredibly daring style.

The Château at Chantilly *contains very valuable collections of paintings (Raphaël, Botticelli, Ingres ...) collected by the Duke of Aumale, fifth son of Louis-Philippe. (Oise.)*

Amiens Cathedral, *the largest gothic building in France, has an astonishing labyrinth depicting meanders, and magnificent 16th century flamboyant stalls. (Somme.)*

Soissons *has retained two major architectural Middle Age religious monuments: the cathedral and abbey of Saint-Jean-des-Vignes, the extremely elegant flamboyant steeples of which can be seen from a distance across the agricultural plain which surrounds the city. (Aisne.)*

Poitou-Charentes

The Poitou area consists of a plain which is drained by the tributaries of the River Loire. Here and there sheep grazed moors are to be seen. Elsewhere the fields and grassland give witness to a prosperous agriculture concentrated upon the raising of beef cattle (Charolais and Limousin), and quality dairy products along with arable production (cereals, and animal fodder).

Saint-Martin-de-Ré, *once the island's fortress, now a charming fishing port, which has kept its ancient alleyways.*

Poitiers, founded during the Gallo-Roman period, has several highly interesting monuments, including the churches of Saint-Hilaire-le-Grand, 1049, and Notre-Dame-la-Grande which is typical of the region's Roman style. The Futuroscope has available the most advanced technology in the field of communications.

Between **Niort** and La Rochelle, the Poitou marsh consisting of a dense network of canals has to be crossed before following the cove of the Aiguillon river which is festooned with oyster and mussel beds. **La Rochelle**, located between Nantes and Bordeaux faces the Atlantic Ocean and has traded with Canada, Louisiana, and the West Indies since the 18th century. Today, trawlers and pleasure boating, for which the port of Minimes has been fitted out, enliven the maritime scene.

The entrance to the **port at La Rochelle**, *a protestant stronghold when the wars of religion, from 1562 to 1598, tore the country apart is defended by the Chain and Saint Nicolas towers. Entrance to the city is via the Clock Tower Gate. (Charente-Maritime.)*

Sainte-Radegonde church at Talmont-sur-Gironde, *at the end of the fortified headland is representative of the Roman saintongeais style with its elegant chevet complimented by buttress columns. (Charente-Maritime.)*

The region of Charentes includes the old provinces of Saintonge (around **Saintes**), Angoumois (around Angoulème), and Aunis (around La Rochelle). The thirty kilometre long **island of Ré** is connected to the mainland by a huge bridge. The inhabitants of the island take full advantage of an exceptionally mild climate, producing excellent early fruit and vegetables, and long beaches bordered with pine trees attract visitors. More to the south, the island of **Oléron** charms with its wooded dunes, its beaches, and white houses.

Saintes (Roman arenas, the Abbey aux Dames), **Cognac** (the vineyards and wine storage) and **Angoulème** (the Roman cathedral), deserve visiting in depth.

Off the coast of Oléron island is **Fort Boyard** *which was constructed for surveillance of the mouth of the River Charente. It is now used as a location for filming a very popular T.V. game. (Charente-Maritime.)*

Green Venice, *to the west of the Poitou marshes, is criss-crossed by a network of canals which encircle cultivated plots. Numerous villages and hamlets have a landing stage, the point of departure for a visit to the marsh. (Deux-Sèvres.)*

Cognac *is a universally well known liqueur, distilled from light, flavoured wines. At Cognac one can visit large storehouses where the subtle alchemy of the alcohol and the oak of the casks results in the ageing of and assemblage of this precious liquid. (Charente.)*

The vaults of the ancient **abbey church of Saint Savin** *are decorated with a remarkable collection of paintings done around 1100, the largest in France. (Vienne.)*

The facade of the church of Notre Dame la Grande at Poitiers *has admirable sculpted decoration, intense life animation and depiction of the Incarnation. The church, by its proportions, is representative of Poitiers' school of Roman art. (Vienne.)*

The Cathedral of Saint Pierre at Angoulême *has a highly decorated sculpted facade which is characterised by the superimposition of arches. The whole decorated by friezes of leaves, medallions, and all varieties of animals, is full of the effect of movement. (Charente.)*

Provence-Alpes-Côte d'Azur

Provence, crossed by the lower waters of the River Rhône, is punctuated by the outlines of the Baronnies, Ventoux, Luberon, Alpilles, Sainte-Victoire, and Sainte-Baume heights. The plains are fully cultivated: fruit, and vegetables in the Comtat Venaissin and Petite Crau areas, vines and olive trees at the foot of the Luberon and the Alpilles, with rice in the Camargue region.

Orange (the Roman theatre), **Avignon** (the Papal Palace), **Arles** (arenas, the cloister of Saint-Trophime) and **Aix-en-Provence** (the Mirabeau square, the Place d'Albertas) are first ranking cities of art. The **Camargue,** at the heart of the Rhône delta, consists of lakes where pink flamingos stroll, and of sandy marshes roamed by herds of horses and wild cattle.

The Cistercian abbeys of Sénanque, Silvacane, and Thoronet, are interesting examples of restrained line Romanesque art.

Founded in the year 600 B.C. by the Phocaeans, **Marseilles**, throughout the centuries, has become one of the most important ports in the Mediterranean. The picturesque Vieux Port is overlooked by the Basilica of Notre-Dame-de-la-Garde.

The Abbey at Sénanque, *founded in 1148, nestles in the hollow of a lavender carpeted valley. It belongs to the considerable Cistercian order, in the same capacity as Silvacane and Le Thoronet (p. 82), its "sisters in the south of France". (Vaucluse.)*

The French Riviera (Côte d'Azur), is a point where the sea, mountains, and the sun meet marking out from **Toulon** to **Menton** a succession of dazzling beaches: with creeks, the Maures and Esterel Massifs, the gulf of Saint-Tropez, the Baie des Anges, the Riviera corniche. **Toulon**, protected by its harbour, is a major naval installation. Since the 1950s **Saint-Tropez** has been a resort of international fame, whilst **Nice**, "pearl" of the French Riviera, has a pebble beach bordered by the Promenade des Anglais along which are established the most luxurious of hotels.

Towards the north, the Alpes-de-Haute-Provence remain southern in character, whilst the massifs of the Mercantour, Queyras and Ecrins have numerous possibilities for ramblers and skiers. The highest city in Europe, **Briançon**, and gateway to the winter sports resort of Serre-Chevalier, has retained its network of fortifications. **Gap**, at the centre of a vast basin, has grown up at the junction of major communications.

The Island of Port Cros, *a classified national park, is without fear of contradiction literally one of Europe's points of paradise.*
It has an exceptional wealth of Mediterranean fauna and flora. Vehicles are forbidden, and visiting by foot is made easy by numerous indicated paths. A few discrete bays are suitable for bathing. (Var.)

The Dentelles de Montmirail, *at the foot of Mount Ventoux, are formed by curious crests of limestone standing erect in the middle of vineyards. They inspire painters, and attract numerous strollers. (Vaucluse.)*

Thoronet Abbey *is not far from the Argens valley, in the middle of wooded hills. Built during the second half of the 12th century its buildings are an example of Cistercian architectural sobriety. (Var.)*

The Colorado de Rustrel, *not far from Apt, is formed from ancient ochre quarries , a mixture of sandy clay and iron oxide. The Vaucluse produces 3,000 tons of ochre annually. this is used in the preparation of paint, and distemper. (Vaucluse.)*

Albertas Square
(17th and 18th centuries), historic centre of Aix-en-Provence. (Bouches-du-Rhône.)

The Roman Theatre at Vaison-la-Romaine, *which can accommodate 6,000 spectators. (Vaucluse.)*

80,000 spectators came to view the gladiators fight in the **Arles Arenas** *built during the reign of Augustus. (Bouches-du-Rhône.)*

The old village of **Baux de Provence** *Citadel in the Alpilles. (Bouches-du-Rhône.)*

Seasonal migration in the Clarée Valley, *near Briançon, which has without doubt the most balanced and hospitable of landscapes in the Dauphinoise mountain area. (Hautes-Alpes.)*

The Esterel Massif seen from Cabris, *near Grasse. Like the Maures Massif, more to the east, for the most part it is covered with fire threatened forests (pine, oak). (Alpes-Maritimes, Var.)*

Saint-Véran, *in the Queyras area, is the highest village in Europe. At more than 2,000 metres, its chalets are grouped together on a well exposed south facing terrace. (Hautes-Alpes.)*

Villefranche-sur-Mer, *both a fishing port and seaside resort, it is located in the hollow of a magnificent harbour overlooked by wooded hills. It has kept its citadel, built at the end of the 16th century by the Duke of Savoy, and the old streets around the marina. (Alpes-Maritimes.)*

During the International Film Festival, in May, cinema lovers and photographers wait in front of **Cannes' palace** *like hotels for the appearance of big screen stars. (Alpes-Maritimes.)*

CARLTON HOTEL
CARLTON

Rhône-Alpes

The Northern Alpes which cover the historical regions of Savoy and the Dauphiné are an area of majestic summits and huge glaciers. At 4,808 meters Mont-Blanc is both the highest peak in the European alpine chain, and that with the most varied relief (the Midi Peak, the Sea of Ice). During summer, then in winter, mountain climbers, ramblers, and skiers never tire of taking the more daring paths, the uncountable tracks and the vast areas for skiing which mark out the region's mountains. Several natural parks (Bauges, Vanoise, Chartreuse, Vercors, Ecrins) attempt to preserve this unique environment.

Located at the confluence of the Isére and the Drac, **Grenoble** has become the financial and intellectual capital of the Alpes. **Chambéry, Aix-les-Bains**, and **Annecy**, close to the Bourget and Annecy lakes ensure their inhabitants an enviable lifestyle.

At the foot of the Alpes lies Dombes a clay plateau scattered with hundreds of lakes.

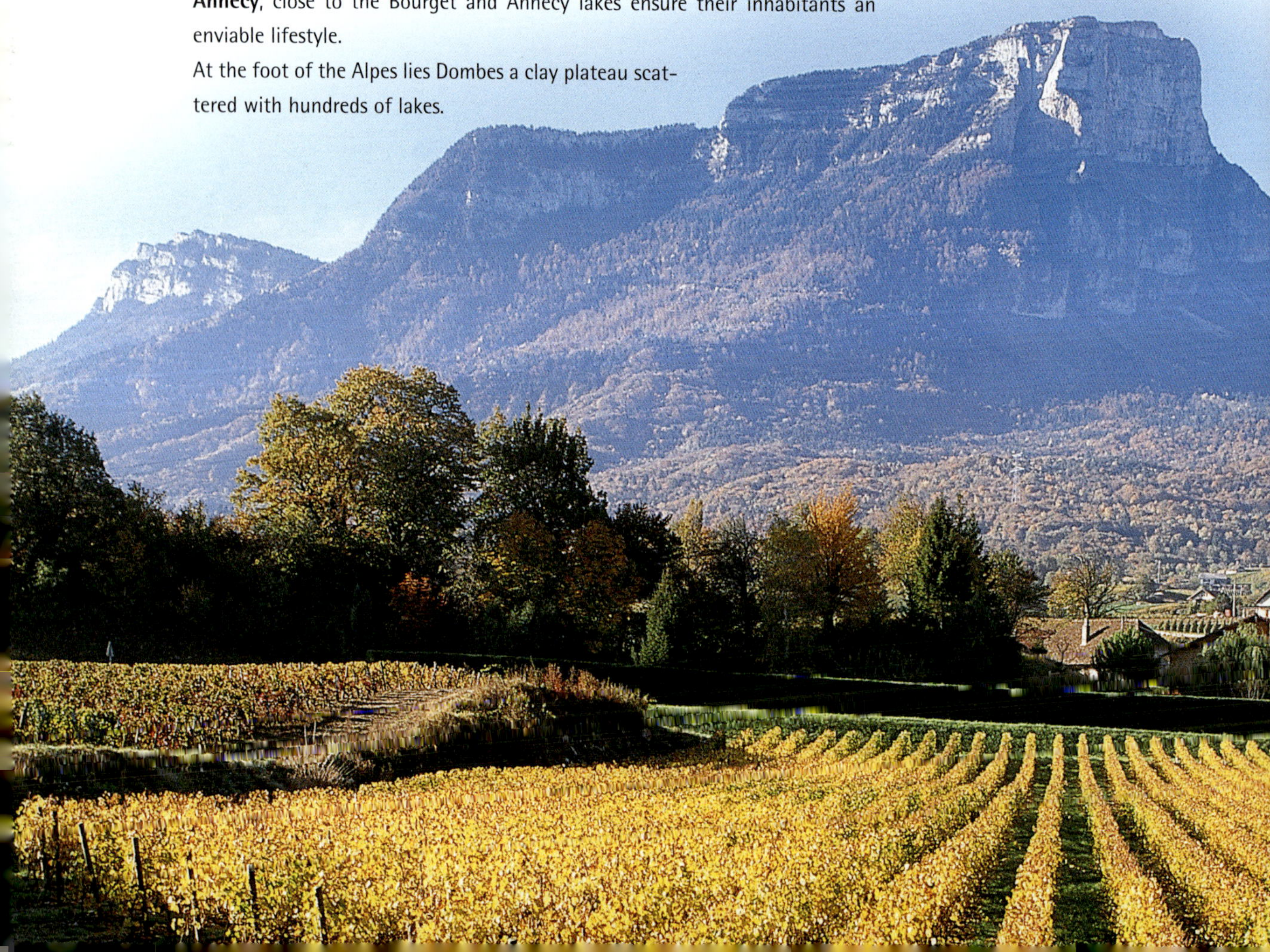

Beyond the Saône river the heights of Beaujolais are covered with vines which produce a fresh fruity red wine. Further to the west, at Forez, verdant fields and grass lands are to be found up to a height of 1,000 meters, above are forests of pine and beech, and high stripped stubble. **Saint-Etienne** is to be found at the start of the Forez plain, it has ceased mining for coal, and diversified its activities.

Lyon, superbly located where the River Rhône and Saône meet has taken advantage of its geographical position to become a prosperous regional metropolis, and first ranking university and medical research establishment.

From Valentinois to the Montélimar basin, the Rhône Valley alternates, between orchards and vineyards, in a huge cultivated patchwork.

To the south of Valence, the Rhône runs between the Vivarais, at the edge of the Massif Central shaped by erosion (numerous natural curiosities) and the Vercors, a high limestone plateau hollowed out by water.

The Vercors, *a high limestone plateau, was gouged by rivers. Roads are sometimes dug even into the sides, and numerous paths for strolling criss-cross the mountain. (Isère, Drôme.)*

At the foot of Mount Granier, *on the eastern exposed slopes which overlook the River Isère, thrives a vast vineyard which takes advantage of the first rays of the sun. (Isère, Savoie.)*

The Midi Peak *(3,842 metres) launches its formidable wall of rock above the Chamonix valley.(Haute-Savoie.)*

Between Vercors and Provence, the Diois massif consists of a succession of crests and hollows. (Drôme.)

Between the valleys of Romanche and Vénéon, the **Deux-Alpes** *have a huge area for skiing, and lots of sunshine for skiers. (Isère.)*

The Gorges de l'Ardèche *which can be visited by canoe, or kayak, have profoundly eaten into the plateau of the lower Vivarais. (Ardèche.)*

Between the rivers Saône and Loire, **Charlieu** has for a long time played an important commercial role. Today the city is specialised in the weavimg of silk, and the hosiery trade. Its Benedictine abbey, founded in 870, then incorporated into Cluny, had its Roman cloister rebuilt during the 15th century.

On the hillsides which overlook the River Saône, *to the north of Lyon, the grape has been cultivated since Roman times. They produce fruity, red, wines which are best drank when young. The Beaujolais Villages exists as follows: Morgon, Chiroubles, Juliénas, Moulin-à-vent, Fleurie, Chénas, Côte-de-Brouilly, Brouilly, Régnié, and Saint-Amour. Before the development of improved means of transport, Lyon, was the main outlet for this wine, to the point that the city was, as the joke goes is, "watered by three rivers: the Rhône, the Saône, and the Beaujolais". (Saône-et-Loire.)*

The cathedral of Saint Jean at Lyon, *se commenced during the 12th century, has a gothic facade the portals of which have retained a very omate early 14th century decor. (Rhône.)*

The choir of Brou Church *(suburbs of Bourg-en-Bresse), built by Margaret of Austria from 1506, houses numerous tombs which mark the high point of Flemish sculpture in Burgundy. Tomb of Margaret of Austria. (Ain.)*

Overseas france

Guadeloupe and Martinique, each of which being separate regions, are volcanic islands located between the Atlantic ocean and the Caribbean. Apart from the exotic clichés about the beaches, coconut trees, and West Indian music, they are endeavouring to add to the resources of tourism by economic diversification to compensate for the slow decline in sugar cane.

To the north of Brazil, beside the Atlantic, **Guyana** is, for the most part, covered with tropical forest. Its subsoil is rich (bauxite, gold) and tourism is in the process of being developed. The Aerospace Centre at Kourou is responsible for launching the Ariane European Rocket.

The island of **Réunion** is located in the Indian Ocean, off shore from Madagascar. It is characterised by its volcanic outline (Piton de la Fournaise, 2,631 meters), and a temperate tropical climate suitable for the cultivation of sugar cane, vanilla, and plants for the manufacture of perfume. Magnificent scenery, and the attraction of the sea make it a favourite destination for tourists throughout the entire year.

Off the coast of Réunion, *a dive under a sea of incredible wealth. (La Réunion.)*

Ph. E. Dutrieux.

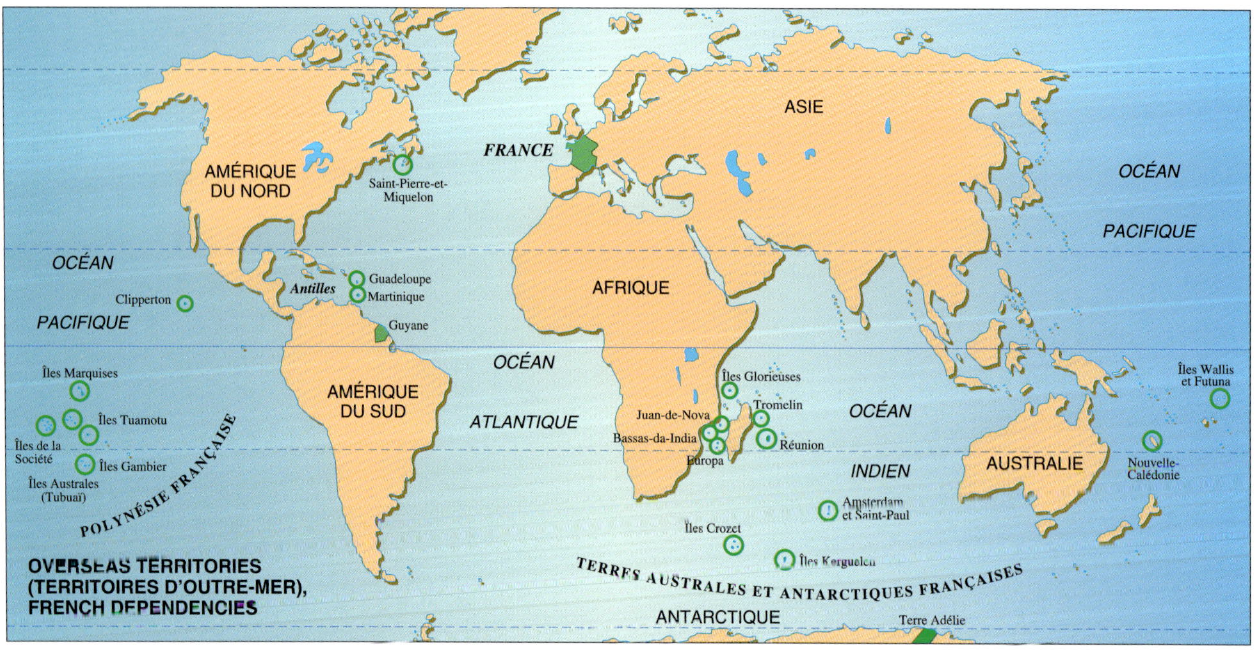

Off the coast of Guadeloupe, **the Saintes' archipelago** *has kept intact the ma or part of its idyllic landscape. (Guadeloupe.)*

Overseas Territories include **New Caledonia**, Melanesian islands whose main resources, other than tourism, are nickel and forestry, **Polynesia** with Tahiti and the Marchesas with idyllic landscapes, and **Mayotte**, small island in the Comoros in the Indian Ocean.

Anses-d'Arlets, *facing the Caribbean, is a charming fishing village which has retained its traditional huts. (Martinique.)*

index

First cover page: *Etretat Cliffs (Seine-Maritime.) ; Château de Chambord (Loir-et-Cher.) ; Sacré-Cœur (Paris) ; Sénanque Abbey (Vaucluse); Pays de Cize in the Basque country (Pyrénées-Atlantiques.)*

Fourth cover page: *Cantal; Saint-Florent (Corsica); les Dentelles de Montmirail. (Vaucluse.)*

Cartography: Patrick Mériennc - Photogravure: Nord Compo, Villeneuve d'Ascq

Cet ouvrage a été achevé d'imprimer par l'imprimerie Pollina, Luçon (85) - n° L99521
I.S.B.N. 2.7373.2806.3 - N° d'éditeur : 4182.04.1,5.02.06
Dépôt légal : mars 2001